BOOST YOUR BUSINESS IN ANY ECONOMY

BOOST YOUR BUSINESS IN ANY ECONOMY

Bill Gibson

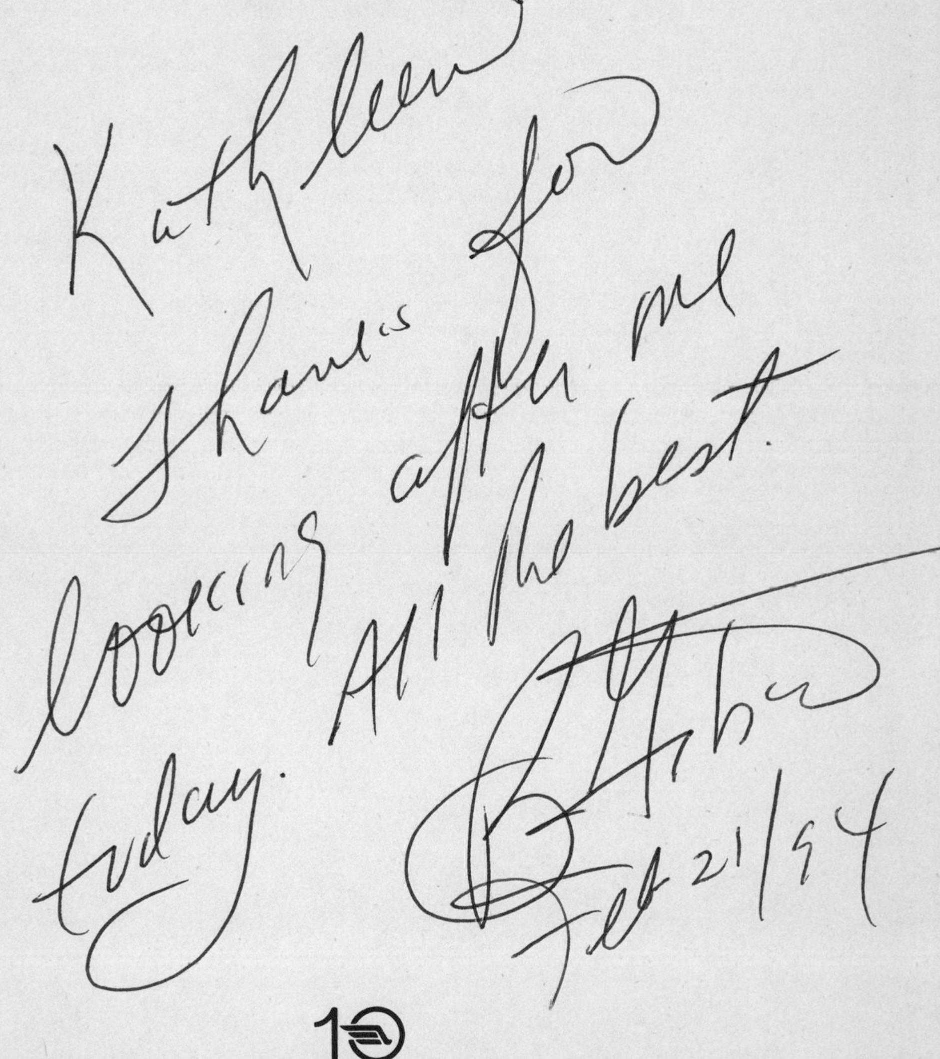

TEN SPEED PRESS
Berkeley, California

Excerpt from *America in the 1990's* copyright © 1992 by David Pearce Synder and Gregg Edwards (Washington, D.C.: American Society of Association Executives). Reprinted with kind permission of the authors.

Excerpt from "Growing Concerns—The Five Stages of Business Growth" (*Harvard Business Review*, May–June 1983) by Neil C. Churchill and Virginia L. Lewis, copyright © 1983 by Harvard Business Review. Reprinted with kind permission of the publisher.

Excerpt from "Consumers Deeper in Debt" (*The Financial Post*, May 17, 1988) copyright © 1988 by The Financial Post. Reprinted with kind permission of the publisher.

Excerpt from "Bad Times Are Golden for Enterprising Firms" (*Toronto Star*, January 25, 1992) by Barbara Aarsteinsen, copyright © 1992 by The Toronto Star Syndicate. Reprinted with kind permission of the publisher.

Excerpt from "Keep Your Eye on the Track" (*FORBES*, January 6, 1992) by Fleming Meeks, copyright © 1992 by FORBES magazine. Reprinted with kind permission of the publisher.

Ten Speed Press
P.O. Box 7123
Berkeley, California 94707

Cover design by Fifth Street Design

Text design and typography by Publication Services, Inc.

FIRST TEN SPEED PRESS PRINTING 1993

Library of Congress Cataloging-in-Publication Data

Gibson, Bill, 1945-
Boost your business in any economy / Bill Gibson.
p. cm.
ISBN 0-89815-516-9 : $9.95
1. Business. 2. New business enterprises. 3. Entrepreneurship.
I. Title.
HF5351.G46 1992
658.4'06–dc20 92-23220
CIP

Printed in the United States of America
2 3 4 5 – 97 96 95 94 93

ACKNOWLEDGMENTS

Boost Your Business in Any *Economy* is a product of more than twenty years of working with literally hundreds of small and large businesses throughout North America. The book is packed with the personal lessons I've learned as an entrepreneur and dozens of true stories of businesspeople who have mastered the process of boosting their business in any economy.

First, I'd like to thank Beverley, my wife, partner, and friend, for unwavering faith and support. This book would not have been possible if you had not boldly held down the home front while I criss-crossed North America gathering the stories and experiences that enabled me to write this "timely" book. I'd also like to thank my two sons and business partners, Shane and Ryan Gibson, who are now sixteen and thirteen years old, respectively. Your maturity has been a great inspiration to me. You are great friends, sons, and advisors. And to Frank Krancevic, thanks for helping out with the boys as a friend and brother while I was away.

Thanks to Uncle Reid Shanks for my first job as a gas attendant in your service station. Without your support in my young entrepreneur days, I wouldn't be working for myself today.

To Mary and Murray Gibson, my Mom and Dad, and my older sister Sharon, thanks for the principles that have put me back on my feet time and time again. To Betty and Don McCarthy, my mother- and father-in-law, thanks for the help when I needed it. And thank you for such a lovely wife.

Special mention to Bill and Jennifer Johnson, who initially did all the work from 1982 to 1984 and made sure that people showed up for the original *Boost Your Business in* Any *Economy* events. Those towns have never been the same. And thanks to Neil Godin—together we created a lot. I hope you are proud of what we accomplished. It is my pleasure to have you as a friend.

Thanks to Eileen Fitzpatrick, who cheerfully rolled with the punches in the budding years at Newport. We miss you! And thanks to Greg Ioannou and his associates, Lynne Missen and Tracy Bordian, at The Editorial Centre in Toronto. You've worked hard. All the false stops and starts were not easy, and, as you've discovered, it isn't easy to second guess me. You've done well. Thanks.

To Marilyn Hamilton, thank you for pushing me to keep the *Business Advisor Newsletter* going. The articles I had written really helped save me time and the real-life stories collected by you and the other Newport business advisors were invaluable.

To the network of Newport business advisors who worked with me over the past five years, you are all great. Good luck! And to Terry Straker, Rick Gibson-Shaw, and Bob Davidson, who lent me two days of brainpower, check out the book—you'll see yourselves everywhere.

To Mike Pals, Wayne Forster, Rick, Terry, Tim, and Steve, thanks for continuing the Newport programs. And to Peter Gray, thank you for standing guard and giving me breathing room to work on this book.

To Ten Speed, it has been a pleasure working with you. And to Jeff Herman, and Vance Schafer, your guidance has been appreciated.

To Jim Rapino of the North West Enterprise Centre, it has been a good relationship. And to all the managers and staff at the Canada Employment Centres who worked with me, I thank you.

To the Chambers of Commerce and Boards of Trade throughout Canada, you've been great allies. And to all the authors, businesspeople, and friends like Dennis Cauvier and Jeff Beaudrey, thanks for the insights.

The acknowledgments are many because *Boost Your Business in* Any *Economy* is the result of a synergy of literally hundreds of people. I'm only the messenger.

TABLE OF CONTENTS

Chapter 1 Riding the Waves of Turbulent Times 1

Understanding Economic Cycles 2
Taking Charge of Your Economy 7
Adapting to Change 9

Chapter 2 Taking Control of Your Own Economy 13

Strategies for Success 13
Innovative Advertising 16
Doing What Is Necessary to Succeed 18
Innovative Merchandising 19
Eight Strategies 20

Chapter 3 Walking on Ceilings 22

The Importance of Research and Brainstorming 23
Making the Most of Your Resources 25
Think Small 27

Chapter 4 Face the Facts 30

The Existence Stage 32
The Survival Stage 33
The Success Stage 33
The Takeoff Stage 35
The Resource Maturity Stage 38
Assessing Where You Are and Moving to the Next Stage 38

Using Information on Stages and Critical Factors 40
Understand these Stages 42

Chapter 5 The Thirty-Minute Snapshot 45

Dealing with Your Opposing Attributes 46
Using the Snapshot to Improve 46
Face the Facts 48

Chapter 6 Commando Thinking 51

Adding to Your Business 53
Improving Sales Meetings 54
Building Relationships 55
Making a Commitment 56
Remaining Innovative 57
Becoming a Commando Thinker 58

Chapter 7 Everyone Needs to Sell 60

The Basics of Selling 61
Business Cards 62
Generating Leads 63
Obtaining Referrals 64
Using the Telephone 66
Networking 68
Other Methods 69
Strategies of an Effective Salesperson 70
Qualifying Buyers 72
Closing the Sale 73
Beyond Technique 74

Chapter 8 United We Stand 77

Dunsmuir Shell 77
The Herzberg Theory 80
Team Commitment 83

Chapter 9 The Royal Treatment 87

People Remember Service 87
Resolving Service Problems 90
Shopping Your Business 92
Personalizing Service 93
Initiating an Effective System 95

Chapter 10 Moving the Market 99

The Importance of Frequency 101
Taking Advantage of the Media 103
Obtaining the Right Information 106
Directing Your Advertising 107
The Message 111
Managing Your Budget 114
Promotional Events 115

Chapter 11 Lean and Keen 116

Cutting the Fat 117
Cutting Staff 118
Being Honest with Your People 120
Business Strategies in Tough Times 121
Making Wise Decisions 123
Other Considerations on Staying Lean 125

Chapter 12 Financially Fit 128

Managing Your Budget 132
Squeezing the Checkbook 135
Collecting Your Money 138
Erasing Your Debt 142

Chapter 13 Mentally Fit 144

Balancing Your Time 145
Reducing Anxieties 145
Tackling Your Problems 157
Dealing With Creditors 158
Thinking Positive 159

Chapter 14 An Inside-Out Summary 164

BOOST YOUR BUSINESS IN ANY ECONOMY

CHAPTER
ONE

Riding the Waves of Turbulent Times

In 1982 I left a senior management position in the broadcast industry to open my own business in Victoria on the west coast of Canada. I had owned several small businesses previously and had consulted for many business enterprises over the years. Like a lot of people starting small companies, I didn't have a lot of money, so I asked myself a question: "Where can I best use my talents and get quick results?"

capitalize on a problem

We were moving into a recession. In fact, we were well into it in North America by 1982. I thought, "What do people need during a recession? They're worried about surviving." So I put together a concept for a business survival seminar. Searching for business opportunities in this way is called *capitalizing on a problem*.

boldness

I ran an ad in the *Sun* and the *Province* newspapers in Vancouver, British Columbia. To my amazement there were only two responses to the ads, and not surprisingly they were both from the government. Joe McKay from the British Columbia Ministry of Small Business Development called me up to see if I was serious about doing the business survival seminar. I told him that I most certainly was serious, and I gave him a little background on my concept. He asked me if I had a workbook. "Do you need one?" I asked. He said yes. "Then I have one." He asked if I could send him a copy. "Not right now. It's at the printers," I answered. There was a silence, and then we both began to chuckle. I then told him the truth (very important). "Joe, if you need one I could have it together in seven days, but it is in my head right now." "Great. Send it over," he said. He then complimented me for the way I strung him along about the workbook and said that they needed someone with courage for this project.

This is called "boldness," and we need it in business. There is nothing wrong with going after a project that you are not completely ready to handle as long as you have the resources to pull it together once you get the job. My philosophy is "If not I, who? If not now, when? If not this way, what way?" If I don't take the job, someone else who is not really qualified will probably get it. I'm sure this has happened to you: someone who is less qualified but happens to be a bit more self-assured has moved past you and gotten the job. In turbulent and changing times we need boldness. My boldness helped me launch a successful career in speaking, consulting, training, and entrepreneurial development.

Understanding Economic Cycles

When Joe saw the workbook he hired me to go to Port Alberni to speak. At the time, Port Alberni was basically a one-industry (forestry) town with an unemployment rate of over 30 percent. The B.C. Ministry of Small Business Development had talked to several other consultants, but none of them wanted to go to Port Alberni to give a survival seminar. I definitely needed the money—and anyway, I'd never spent anytime in Port Alberni. Besides, who would be better qualified for this job than someone who grew up in a small, one-industry community in Atlantic Canada where economic ups and downs were common?

enlist help

Even though my heritage made me tough enough for the job, I decided that I'd be tougher if I had a friend to support me on this challenging assignment. In business it is important to enlist help when facing tough circumstances. So I contacted Neil Godin, a friend who had brainstormed the seminar concept with me. The two of us, armed with nothing but a stack of information and the little workbook we had put together, went to conduct a session called Business Survival with the community of Port Alberni. Fifty people showed up.

Later, Neil and I discovered that more people would have attended if the session had not been titled Business Survival. Who wants to be seen at a business survival seminar? In other communities we changed the title to How to Boost Your Business in *Any* Economy. Then we packed the house. (You don't have to worry about this book on your desk because smart businesspeople are always looking for ways to boost their businesses in *any* economy.)

understand the climate

In Port Alberni, our strategy (besides delivering dozens of innovative, inexpensive ways to boost sales and survive) was to explain how economic cycles work. If you understand something, you feel a lot better about it. The reason so many of us get uptight about bad times is that we don't understand what is going on. If you understand the basic economic cycles, then you are better able to react to a downward swing. And if you understand how the general economic climate affects your business—as well as how it *doesn't*—then you'll be better equipped for riding the waves of even the stormiest economies. The good news for the folks in Port Alberni was that they were at the bottom—and there was nowhere to go but up.

That night, Neil and I delivered lots of down-to-earth, easy-to-use materials to the people of Port Alberni. We also provided lots of business-related skits to add humor so the participants could relax, enjoy, and absorb. One of the things I told them that night, and still tell people today, is "If you own a business, you should laugh a lot—because some years the only thing that you may get from your business is a good laugh." I'm sure you can appreciate the truth in this statement.

over-bought

Let's begin by considering what Neil and I had to say about economic cycles and how it still applies to everyone today. At the top of the economic cycle, our society is overbought. This means that people have bought and spent at a very high rate. If the newspapers state that the ratio of consumer debt to income is going higher and higher, that's a good sign of an overbought society. (Every business should have an ongoing file of newspaper and magazine clippings that track the economy. The file should include consumer debt ratios, interest rates, changing banking philosophies, and the like. This way you can watch the signs of the times. If you are approaching the top of the economic cycle, put cash aside for tight times so you can take advantage of opportunities on the downswing. In a down economy, cash is king.)

When our society is overbought, we reach a point where people won't, can't, or don't need to buy any more. For example, two-and-a-half years ago I bought a beautiful Lincoln. Last year, my wife bought a Volvo. This year we have been approached two or three times by people in the car business asking, "Why don't you buy a new car?" But we don't need a new car; we already have two—both still fairly new. Someone else tried to sell me a videocassette recorder, but I already have two VCRs, and so on.

debts build and spending slows

Business purchases work the same way. We get one cellular phone, and then we decide we need two. We buy a new photocopier, then a fax machine, and we keep adding and adding. Businesses everywhere are adding, and the business equipment companies are having a boom. But somewhere along the line it has to stop, and usually at this point the financial institutions help you and me stop spending—they cut us off!

Suddenly, we reach a point where business and consumers don't need to spend money on anything new, and the economy begins to slow. People are in debt, and the banks are starting to look at their loans and cut down credit limits. We've seen the results in both Canada and the United States: Credit slows down and cash begins to dry up.

too much inventory

If you're in business, you have probably been producing at your peak, perhaps even expanding to keep up with the fast market. Suddenly, the market's not there, and you have to slow down production. This leads to bulging inventories. By *inventory*, in this context, I don't just mean automobiles sitting out in a parking lot or widgets in a warehouse; if you're in the service business, your inventory is your people. If you've been hiring lots of people to keep up with all the business, then once things begin to slow down, you've got people that you don't need—bulging inventories. People who've been around for a while have seen this before. They think, "Oh, oh! This looks familiar, we'd better move out some of this inventory." So prices begin to slip to help move the inventory, wages get cut, or people get laid off.

negative news

At this point the news media become a factor in the economic cycle. Negative news begins to appear on the television, on the radio, and in the newspapers. It's something to grab on to. Now that the boom is old news, they grab on to the bad news, accentuate it, and milk it for all they can. Negative news sells. (If someone is unhappy with your service, they tell eleven people, but if they are happy they only tell three.)

loss of confidence

Because of this initial negative news, a little worry sets in, buying dries up a bit more, and we get more negative news. Businesses and consumers start to lose confidence. Government loses confidence. Labor loses confidence. Once confidence is gone, layoffs begin. A little more worry, a few more layoffs.

In the meantime, however, savings begin to build. During the economic downturn in 1981 to 1982, for example, there was more money in the average Canadian savings account than ever in the history of the country. The fact is that during a recession, there is not a whole lot less money around—just a whole lot less confidence. The building of savings and the reduction of the debts in the United States changed substantially from 1990 to 1991 in the average U.S. home—another recession.

money stops spinning

Think about it. If the unemployment rate jumps from, say, 7 to 10 percent, 3 percent fewer people are employed. Most of these people can collect unemployment insurance, so they still have incomes. But someone receiving unemployment insurance feels a lot less secure than someone with a job, naturally. So people don't consume as much; the money that *is* there doesn't reach the market. Everybody gets nervous and cautious.

In such an atmosphere, the money doesn't spin, which means the money doesn't generate as much additional financial activity as it would in times of optimism. In a tourist city on the coast, for instance, a group was able to research how many times a dollar spun in their economy. They determined that if a person visiting the city spent $100, a dollar would spin four-and-a-half times before stopping. That means that this $100 really injects $450 into the economy. When the money stops spinning, the economy really slows down. During slow times or times when people lose confidence, a dollar might spin only a couple of times. This has a real impact. A lot less money is being spent even though there is just as much net money around.

excessive pessimism

As the slowdown continues, you get even more negative news in the media. It may start to look like the economy is going to fall apart, so we really put the brakes on money. People are afraid, and the result of that fear is usually panic. (Remember, though, that because people are buying less, savings continue to build.)

When an entire country is ready to panic, people begin selling at huge discounts and cutting the meat instead of the fat. Everybody is bailing out because they're not sure what to do. People's minds are scrambled; they are not really organized. We have hit the bottom of the economic cycle, and you can tell this by the excessively pessimistic atmosphere. When everybody is bailing out, start buying and marketing because the economy is ready to go up. The best time to gain market share is at the bottom, when your competitors are immobilized by negative news or have gone out of business. Wouldn't you rather compete with a tennis player, wrestler, or gymnast who is depressed and has not worked out for a long time? If you are in top shape at the bottom of the economy, you've got the edge.

When you are at the top of the economic cycle, everybody is excessively optimistic. When you hear comments such as "There is no way that you can lose in real estate"; "Buy now—this thing is going to double in the next two years"; "Hey, get in on the action in the stock market"; or "This is the greatest country in the world with all this money coming in from Asian countries," you know that we are probably at the top. Batten down the hatches and move with realism. When you hear comments such as "We are going to hell in a hand basket"—I read those exact words in the *Globe and Mail* in 1990—then we are, without a doubt, darn close to the bottom.

make your move at the bottom

Frequently at my seminars I ask, "How many people have gone into business in the last seven years?" Usually at least 60 or 70 percent of the people in the audience raise their hands. They are fairly new in business and have probably never experienced an economic cycle as an owner. They get caught by surprise. But those who have been around for a while recognize the signs. As soon as it gets to the bottom, we say, "It's low enough. Let's go out and make some good investments. Let's start hiring the good people who are available. Let's grab the market share."

The main headline in the *Saturday Star* in Toronto on January 25, 1992, at the bottom of a heavy recession, was "Bad times are golden for enterprising firms." In the article, Barbara Aarsteinsen reports:

The company [music seller HMV Canada] made a splash when it arrived and has doggedly maintained that momentum, refusing to let up even when the economy started to sink.

Now's the time to ruthlessly make inroads against rivals, professes Alofs, a Windsor, Ont., native with a marketing background.

Retail analysts agree, forecasting that HMV, which has a hold on slightly more than 15 percent of the domestic music market, will soon be neck and neck with industry leader Sam the Record Man, whose share has slipped to less than 20 percent.

"Alofs is a marathoner," says consultant Len Kubas. "He is using this period of turbulence to his benefit. I have no doubt that he will soon pass the competition."

Alofs increased HMV's promotional spending in 1991 and intends to lavish bigger bucks in 1992—including an undisclosed six figure sum on market research alone.

He has increased the chain's advertising budget and turned increasingly to the print media and direct mail, believing consumers want information, not hype.

HMV is including more text in its ads, is making use of customer testimonials and has started distributing an in-store magazine.

With consumers likewise becoming value-conscious, HMV is introducing more "listening posts" to its stores, giving patrons a chance to try out music before they buy.

The chain has a frequent buyer club, and it is watching its pricing closely. The store launches this weekend, for example, a year-long CD sale, in which ninety-two disks from across the spectrum will be offered for $9.92 each.

Alofs has also used the recession to cut better real estate deals and recruit good employees.

HMV has always allowed individual managers to make their own decisions on everything from pricing to hiring. Alofs has continued to flatten the management structure even more, banishing an entire layer of executives from the head office and sending them into the field.

The news media start with a few small stories such as this one, which prompts a few more people to gain confidence and begin spending. This is the beginning of the turnaround. A little more buying kicks in, then a little more positive news, and then a little more confidence. People begin to think, "My gosh, this looks like it's for real—let's get in on it." People invest, they put energy into projects, there is a little more buying, and soon prices start to rise. There is a fear of higher prices, which really starts to move the market on the upswing. That's really positive news.

Then comes a period of real demand, a scramble to produce, a scramble to buy—and then over the top we go again.

learning from history

If you think this is something new, just look at this history of economic bottoms since 1949:

- In 1949 to 1950 the economy was declared to be a general disaster; it turned around and took off again.
- In 1957 the U.S. Treasury Secretary, George Humphrey, said, "The coming depression will curl your hair." As soon as he made that statement, the economy rebounded.

- In 1962 the repeat crash was imminent; there was no doubt. At the same time the Cuban missile crisis erupted. But once again, the economy turned around.
- In 1970 Penn Central went bankrupt. When you hear of such things—a major railroad company in the United States going bankrupt—it seems as if it's all over for the rest of us. Chrysler was also on the brink of bankruptcy. To add to the turbulence, there was Vietnam and Cambodia, student riots, and other troubles. People were wondering where North America was going. However, as those events unfolded, the economy boomed again.
- In 1974 and 1975 we saw the worst decline since 1929: double-digit inflation and an oil embargo. A poll showed that half of all people expected a depression in the United States and Canada. The economy turned around and took off again.
- The 1981 to 1982 recession was even worse. We didn't know whether we could weather the storm. Up we went again.
- In 1991 we hit the bottom again during the Gulf War and the breakup of the Soviet Union. And now signs are indicating a slow recovery.

It's amazing that, given the cyclical nature of this process, people always panic when an economy heads downward. Experience, as well as logic, has shown that the trend is never permanent but instead is part of a natural cycle of our economies. The bottoms of the economy since 1949 to 1950 were from five to eight years apart. You can almost set your clock by the market cycles.

set your clock by market bottoms

Taking Charge of Your Economy

You can have similar economic cycles in your own business. When, in your own operation, everybody is excessively optimistic about everything—saying "Go for the gusto" and "This thing will never stop"—you may need a note of caution. You could be spending too much money and energy and may find yourself in a tight spot when you reach the end of your own boom. Look around carefully—there may be some problems you've been ignoring. On the other hand, if things look excessively pessimistic, you are probably at the bottom of a swing. You should be going back up soon. Many people experience a personal boom economy when the big economy is at the bottom and have a bust when the big economy is booming. That explains why there are still bankruptcies at the top of an economic cycle.

Once you realize that no economy, large or small, ever *stays* down, you can actually find many ways to benefit from the downswings. The key is to *take charge of your own economy*. Don't worry about all the events around

take charge of your own economy

you—you can't do anything about them. The question is: What can you do about yourself and your situation?

you can't average one

Don't be scared by statistics. However low the economy sinks, remember that you can't average one. Although your position is part of the economic average, *you cannot be controlled by the average in any way, because you are just one*. Think about it. If your industry is down 30 percent in sales, that doesn't mean everyone is down 30 percent. It probably means that some people are down 65 or 70 percent and some people are up 5 or 10 percent. That's how you get an average of minus 30. So make sure *yours* is the company that's up. An average is the best of the worst and the worst of the best. Who wants to be average? Whatever the average, be the part that's at the top, pulling the average up; that's the goal for running a business in turbulent times.

In both Canada and the United States, there has been a definite downturn and a bottoming out of the economy; this is obviously on everybody's mind when we use the term *turbulent times*. But let's stop and think more about what's meant by "turbulent."

what are turbulent times

In 1989 the Berlin Wall came down; that is turbulence. Since then, Iraq invaded Kuwait; free elections sprang up all over Eastern Europe; major trading blocks have been set up throughout the world; the Soviet Union has dissolved; and Margaret Thatcher resigned after twelve years in power in England. I've changed this paragraph five times in the nine months it took me to write this book, and there will have been other turbulent changes in the world by the time you read it.

Then there are demographic changes. I have recently heard that in Canada for every person who is turning twenty-one, approximately two people are turning fifty. I expect the figures are similar in the United States. The decline in new workers entering the work force is phenomenal—from 300,000 in 1990 to a predicted 200,000 by the end of the century in Canada, and ratios are similar in the United States. No wonder government is opening up the borders to attract immigrants. We need workers.

Additionally, there are critical environmental issues. Ten years ago, *environment* was little more than a buzz word. Today, however, the importance of environmental issues is recognized by almost everyone.

Our outlook on education and a lot of things in life has changed. I have a sixteen-year-old son, Shane, who last year was in grade ten in Vancouver. He was in a program called TREK, in which half his year (five months) was academic and the other half was oriented toward outdoor activity. He snow caved, snowshoed, skied, rock climbed, kayaked, learned how to survive in the wilderness and look after our environment, and did community service work. When I did that kind of thing in my youth, it was called playing hookey. People were always trying to get us back into the schoolroom. Now, however, the thinking has changed; education outside the classroom walls is accepted and often encouraged. My son even managed to get me to go on a fifty-mile, six-day wilderness trek, up 300 rung ladders, over rope bridges, and across canyons in hand-pulled, two-seater cable cars on the West Coast trail. Five years ago I wouldn't have thought of it; after the experience it will be another five years before I do it again! What we do to be close to our children these days!

Adapting to Change

According to David Pearce Snyder and Gregg Edwards in their new book, *America in the 1990's* (published in March, 1992 by the American Society of Association Executives), "The 1990s promise a techno-economic revolution. To prosper, you must adapt."

In their opening chapter Snyder and Edwards spell out "seven great realities" of the coming decade:

- ***Reality 1:*** *U.S. productivity has grown slowly for 25 years.*
  Consequence: The standard of living for most U.S. households and sales of U.S. goods and services will decline during the 1990s if we do not substantially improve productivity.
- ***Reality 2:*** *Investment and development in computer and communication technology has set the stage for a decade of powerful and practical new information systems and services.*
  Consequence: Increasingly, economic productivity and personal well-being will depend upon the ability to use information and information technology.
- ***Reality 3:*** *The only consistent way to improve productivity is to bring more and better information to bear on all types of problem solving and decision making.*
  Consequence: The information content of every job will have to be substantially increased.
- ***Reality 4:*** *Techno-economic transitions take one to two generations, during which productivity and general levels of overall prosperity temporarily decline before they rise.*
  Consequence: The 15- to 20-year decline in average weekly wages will continue into the mid-1990s.
- ***Reality 5:*** *A growing number of individuals per household will be forced to seek employment in a job market in which a severe shortage of trainable labor will force employers to hire essentially all people with productive skills.*
  Consequence: To fully employ the wide variety of adults seeking work will require employers to make fundamental changes and innovations in traditional work practices and arrangements.

- ***Reality** 6: Improving U.S. productivity depends upon a substantial increase in the communication, computation, and reasoning skills of all Americans.*
  Consequence: We must substantially improve public school performance, educationally retrieve millions of marginally skilled adults and displaced workers, and improve the skills of current employees.
- ***Reality** 7: Traditional management systems restrict significant discretionary decisions to senior managers and executive positions.*
  Consequence: Massive investments in new workplace technology and human resource development will be largely wasted if we do not also empower employees at all levels to act upon the information at their disposal.

We are faced with so much change that even if the economy happens to be strong, many of us will still experience turbulent times. The concepts and strategies you will learn from this book about how to boost your business are tried and proven, but they are also flexible. Look for ways to transfer the ideas and stories presented here to your business and personal life. Many relate to the economy, as it is a primary consideration for most businesses. However, the trick to riding the waves—in fact, to staying afloat at all—is learning to utilize all your resources in order to react to the continual changes that we are all faced with. A fast-growing company has turbulent times in the areas of systems, people handling, and financing. Less worry and less energy spent chatting about circumstances beyond our control will automatically make us better off at any time.

Following is a list of eight ways to help you continually ride the waves of turbulent and changing times.

1. Post the history of economic bottoms on the wall where you can see it. You may take it from this chapter or create your own. You might also want to create a chart or some other representation of the information presented earlier in this chapter about economic cycles.
2. Start your own economic indicators file as suggested earlier in the chapter. This should include data such as unemployment statistics, interest rates, corporate profits, consumer spending, consumer debt, new home starts, real estate sales, and automobile sales.
3. Review the file and the charts whenever you are making major decisions and/or doing a quarterly review. This is vital information for planning and decision making. Economic indicators may signify we are at the top of the economic cycle. If this is the case, you should wait for the bottom before you expand. Labor will be less expensive, real estate will be cheaper, and interest rates may be lower. A study of this information can tell you when to borrow, when to accumulate

cash, when to raise or lower prices, when to recruit people, and when to get aggressive in your marketing. There will be excellent examples throughout this book that show the possibilities when using this information.

4. Relate excessive optimism (the top) and excessive pessimism (the bottom) not only to the economy, but to yourself, your customers, and your company. There is a big difference between being confident with a positive outlook, and being excessively optimistic. All individuals, departments, companies, and countries have energies that ebb and flow.
5. Make a habit of finding a minimum of three opportunities arising from any situation or circumstance that is news today. For example, three opportunities that could have arisen from the volcanic eruption at Mount Saint Helens in Washington include
    a. Collecting samples of the dust and selling it.
    b. Conducting tours to the site.
    c. Planting trees and cleaning up.

    I am not suggesting that you prey on other people's misfortunes, but I am suggesting that there are several ways to view situations and circumstances. If you make a habit of looking for opportunities in public issues, you will quickly see how to capitalize on your own misfortunes, changes, and turbulent times.
6. If you are near the bottom of the economy (whether going in or out), pull your team together and visualize how immobilized and down your competitors are. Then search for the business opportunity that is being created, and brainstorm all the things you and your team can do to be more productive.
7. Study the "seven great realities" of the future described in this chapter. Make a list of how these realities can affect you positively and negatively, today and in the future. Put a plan together to minimize the negatives and accentuate the positives.
8. Look at change in a positive way. We all know someone in their late sixties, seventies, or eighties who looks as if they are ten to fifteen years younger than they really are. These people are always out participating in new adventures and activities uncommon to their age group. In my opinion, these people have found the fountain of youth. They are not afraid to venture through that awkward growth stage of learning something new. It is much easier to stay secure with the old (an illusion) than to feel awkward, slow, embarrassed, and inadequate while trying the new. However, when you begin to master that new venture, there is a great surge of energy, and that creates spirit. Look

> into the eyes of these active elderly people. You see spirit. They are always learning and progressing.

Individuals, departments, companies, communities, and countries which are willing to accept and tackle change with a vengeance have spirit. Change gives you an opportunity for developing spirit. Turbulent times are changing times—so grab the opportunity to infuse a new energy into yourself and others around you. If you do this, you are well on the way to successfully riding the waves of any turbulent time or situation.

In the following chapters you'll read about ordinary people who successfully took control of their own economic situations, in both smooth and turbulent times by getting their priorities straight. You can do the same by looking at how you can maximize your opportunities at all times. Be ready to change!

Questions to ask yourself:

- Is there another way to look at this problematic situation? If yes, how?
- Who is affected by this problem and how can I create a positive opportunity by helping to solve it?
- Have I or someone I know been in this situation before?
- How did I or someone else solve the problem in the past?
- Regardless of what is happening, what is most important to me right now and what must I do to obtain it?

CHAPTER
TWO

Taking Control of Your Own Economy

To illustrate how you can take control of your own economy and make even the worst situations work for you, let me tell the story of my business associates and personal friends, Terry and Corrine Straker and Forty Winks Waterbeds.

In 1981 in Calgary, I ran a series of advertising seminars. Terry Straker attended one of those sessions. At that time, he and his wife Corrine owned three Forty Winks Waterbed stores in Calgary. After attending my seminar on How To Get Real Action From Every Advertising Dollar, he decided he was wasting a lot of money in advertising; there were a lot of things that he could do to be much more effective.

increase sales by 400%

He hired me to do some consulting. That was when the economy in Calgary was at its absolute peak—it was just starting to dip over. Being a very smart businessperson, Terry realized that a dip in the economy was coming, so we mapped out a strategy to carry him through the bottom part of the cycle. As the economy began to drop, we geared up to take a large market share. When we started working together, Terry's business was number four in the market. Eighteen months later, when we hit the trough of the recession, Forty Winks was by far the number one waterbed chain in the area. Terry had increased his sales by about 400 percent in eighteen months on a downswing. We accomplished this through a number of strategies, many of which involved taking advantage of the low point in the economic cycle.

Strategies for Success

buy right, sell right

First, we undertook a buying strategy. Remember, in a downswing cash is king. We were extremely careful with our inventory control, and we closely watched our cash flow. This allowed us to take advantage of some darn good buys as the economy continued to drop down. We researched our competitors—we literally went and looked at their stores. We saw that many of them were faltering and taking some of the product lines off the floor. We moved in and picked up the good lines at bargain prices. It worked beautifully. Terry was also able to negotiate discounts from many manufacturers by paying in cash. They had cash flow problems because many of the other stores throughout the country were overinventoried and not buying well at the time. The plunging economy made the market a paradise for anyone who could afford to be buying.

tracking results

Next, we tracked our customers. This strategy is useful at any time, but it is especially important in an economic trough—when you need to make every penny you spend count. Each time a sale was made, the salesperson would write down a code that told us the customer's gender and approximate age. (For example, "M2" might mean a male in the second age group, that is, between ages eighteen and thirty-four.) The salespeople would also ask what brought the customer in—TV, radio, newspaper, our sign, the yellow pages, whatever. If it was a newspaper ad, they would ask which one; if it was a TV ad, they would try to find out which station. They even obtained customers' addresses on virtually every sale. The information in these very, very specific records turned out to be extremely valuable.

This information was entered into the computer, and we could access it at any time to find out the exact return on an advertising investment. For example, if we had invested $1,000 in a radio ad that brought in $8,000 worth of sales, the ratio was eight to one. We began to see where we were getting our best returns. When we combined this information with income data from our finance applications, we saw that a specific group of people was buying our beds. Because we knew what brought them in, it was relatively simple to focus on the advertising media that would reach them. We started investing our money only in areas that would give us our best return. The return on investment was phenomenal. The tracking paid off.

Another key to our advertising success was researching the timing of purchases. We wanted to be very careful in spending our money. We looked at the daily sales totals going back two years. When we added up the sales for each day of the month, we found that the majority of purchases were being made in the few days around the end and middle of each month. "Of course," we thought. "Pay days!"

know your best days

The jump at the end of the month was much bigger than the one in the middle. In the last five days of every month, we were doing 50 or 60 percent of the total volume for the month. If this was happening in our business, it had to be happening in all the rest of the waterbed stores in the city. So we decided to concentrate our advertising money at the end of the month. If we blew our whole budget for the month at the right moment, we would pick up more of the market than the other competitors, even though they were spending more money over a full thirty-day period.

I convinced Terry to compress his advertising spending into a six-day period and to spend the majority of it before the end of the first day of the promotion, which we would time to begin at the end of the month. We did not want to let the advertising build to the end of the sale; we wanted to maximize it at the beginning. The idea was to reach the potential buyer at least six times by the first day of the promotion in order to bring a large volume of people through the door. These people would then go out and tell all of their friends and create a ground swell of customers over the next few days. It worked. Our tracking showed that the media brought the most customers in up to day one; from day two to six it was word of mouth.

Terry was a little worried. "What am I going to use for money for the rest of the month?" he asked. However, his sales jumped so high during those few days that we decided to do it again in the middle of the month. Within thirty days he had almost doubled his advertising budget, but the return on investment had quadrupled. We were easily outselling one competitor who was spending $24,000 a month on advertising, while we were only spending $12,000.

We knew the best days to hit, and we kept hitting those days hard. Later, when we completely dominated the market, we found that it was wise to spread out the advertising over the month. However, at the time, what we needed was to hit really hard once a month. That, together with the customer research, made our advertising expenditures incredibly efficient.

We also used the customer research for pricing. We discovered that the average male age eighteen to twenty-four was paying about $450 for a waterbed. That told us that promoting a waterbed to that market at $520, which many of our competitors were doing, was not good enough. The price had to be around $449. On the other hand, pricing the bed at $399 didn't boost sales much.

We knew when people wanted to buy, how much they wanted to pay, and exactly what they were looking for. Now we needed to find out why some people weren't buying.

why don't people buy?

We hired people, mostly students (they're affordable and they're absolutely the best—friendly and enthusiastic) to survey people as they left the store. They would ask, "Did you purchase a waterbed?" If the answer was yes, then the student would ask a few questions about the customer service. But if the answer was no, then the student would try to find out why and would fill out a questionnaire right in the parking lot.

We found out even more from the people who didn't buy than we did from the people who did. We asked, "How likely are you to buy a waterbed soon?" We found out that most people planned to buy one that weekend. In other words, when people were shopping, it was not a matter of *if* they would buy, but *where*. If they didn't buy from us, they would buy somewhere else. The same thing applies to other businesses. Most salespeople say that automobile shoppers are just tire kickers, but the majority will buy a car somewhere within a week.

When we asked why people didn't buy, there were many responses. Often people just didn't like the way they were handled by a particular salesperson. Sometimes it was the selection; people would say, "The person didn't show me the waterbed that I was looking for." In that case we would ask what they were looking for and how much they wanted to spend. In most cases we could have gotten the business. Rarely did we look at one of these questionnaires and think, "Gee, we really couldn't serve that customer." It was usually something we could have handled, so we were able to make some changes that led to many more sales.

sales training

Terry was sorry to find out that one of the things that often put customers off was his salespeople. That started him looking at a different type of sales training, with emphasis on leadership and more personal skills. The staff really needed to know how to sell and how to give superior customer service. In good times or bad, superior service is a strategy that works. But in a slow economy, when people are reluctant to spend, service can make all the difference. Terry learned this from those parking lot interviews. Terry, Corrine, and I continually trained the salespeople. We improved customer service, held meetings, brainstormed, involved the staff, upgraded their skills—the works. The mood was sell, sell, sell, and service, service, service, and track, track, track.

We learned an important lesson—the customer is your greatest resource. Terry used information from his customers and potential customers to improve pricing strategies, advertising, customer service, and so on. It was invaluable.

Innovative Advertising

A stream of innovative advertising ideas also made a big difference for Terry. You can make innovative, high-impact advertising work for you whatever the business climate. For Forty Winks Waterbeds in the 1982 recession, innovative advertising worked wonders, especially on one particularly memorable day.

We were in the absolute trough of the recession, and The Brick was moving into town. The Brick is a high-volume furniture retailer in Canada, which was spending a fortune on television and radio, saying, "Don't buy anything—wait until the end of the month when The Brick opens!"

money always works

Terry and I brainstormed ideas on how to combat The Brick's media blitz. We asked ourselves what would appeal to people in a down economy, and the answer we came up with was simple—money. We couldn't afford to compete with The Brick, so we decided that, instead of spending money on advertising, we would give money away.

free publicity

We decided to give away $5,000 by dropping it from a crane outside one of the waterbed stores. The plan was to drop $500 an hour, in small bills, for ten hours. We kept it a secret until the morning before, then we ran one ad and sent out press releases. It was big news. We got front-page newspaper coverage and made the TV news as well. That's the joy of a really innovative promotion: once it becomes news, you get a great return on that exposure.

The promotion was set for the day The Brick opened—a Saturday morning. When Terry got to work he thought there had been a car accident because he had to park eight blocks away; traffic was all tied up as a result of the promotion. The police were there—it was pandemonium. There were thousands of people there, all waiting for the big money drop. People were hanging off the side of the building with fish nets; others were running around with caps to catch the money—it was insane.

We had somebody dressed in a Mr. Money outfit. Actually, it was Terry's brother, Zack (remember, we were really trying not to spend a lot of money on this). Zack went up in the crane and did the first drop. When you drop $500 in the air, it looks like a million dollars. The crowd just went wild.

It wasn't just money, either. We knew we could get people into the parking lot, but we wanted to be sure we got them into the store. We were trying to sell some waterbeds, after all. So we had stapled a coupon to every bill saying, "Bring this in for a surprise gift." We had all kinds of gifts—candy, mugs, hats, and T-shirts. There was also a coupon for a free waterbed. This is where I think we went too far. If I were ever going to do it again, I would stick to money. We announced the free waterbed over the megaphone, and the combination of all that cash on the first drop and the thought of a free waterbed stapled to one of those dollar bills got the crowd really excited; in fact, the police came and stopped the promotion. So we only made the one drop. We managed to calm the crowd. Terry went outside and explained the situation. He told the crowd that he would donate the remaining $4,500 to charity.

tie-in with charity

He donated the money to the Sunshine Fund of the Calgary *Sun*, and we announced it very quickly. The newspaper was a good choice because it was well publicized. The bottom line was that we had thousands of people there who weren't at The Brick. In that sense, it didn't necessarily matter just how many waterbeds we sold. But it turned out to be the best day Terry had ever had. He sold 200 waterbeds and brought in $156,000. Remember, that was in 1982.

We've always wondered if The Brick sold any waterbeds at all that day. We were smaller, but we stole the show. It also raised our profile for the next year; there were even pictures in the newspaper 150 miles away in Edmonton—the home office of The Brick. We nicked The Brick!

hire a look-alike

Another piece of really creative marketing we used was bringing in Sylvester Stallone's brother, Salvatore (Sal). This was at the time Rocky II was a huge hit. "If you've got Rocky fever, you won't believe your eyes—come see Sal Stallone." He really looks like Sylvester, but of course we were able to hire him for a lot less money. This was a strategy to get huge amounts of publicity at not too high a price.

All kinds of people came to look and say, "It's him." Talk about expanding into new markets—we even had a group of bikers in leather jackets come in. One of them said to Terry, "If this is not Rocky, we are going to tear this place apart." (Luckily, they thought he was great.) I don't know if the bikers bought any waterbeds, but that was another big day for sales. There must have been 100 people in the line. But Terry was ready for the increased volume and had extra cash registers and extra salespeople. If he hadn't been prepared, service would have been slow and he would have lost many potential sales.

handling a crowd

Innovation is great, but it's not enough by itself. You need experience and expertise, and sometimes sheer talent. If you don't have it, you have to be prepared to hire it, which is another thing Terry did.

Doing What Is Necessary to Succeed

hire the expertise

When Terry went to my two-day session on advertising, he couldn't believe his ears. He had one of the best-known ad agencies in town, but they were not using most of the marketing strategies I had discussed. Terry asked, "Can I hire you as my ad agency?" I told him I didn't want to be an ad agency, but I agreed to serve as a consultant and teach his people to set up their own department and do their own buying.

First, we hired Dennis Webb, a young media expert from the United States who had won an Emmy award for his work. We wanted to bring in the best person we could, and we were willing to pay well—$1,000 a day. In a recession period, that was a lot of money. But to get the most out of the cycle, you must be willing to invest in the right areas to get the best return during a down time.

We flew Dennis up once a month from San Diego to produce the commercials and had Terry follow him around to learn everything he could. Terry also took some night courses on television advertising, print media, and so on, and eventually started putting all his own material together. It was worth everything he spent.

make it happen

All during that recession, we kept a very strong focus. Everything was proactive; we didn't wait for anything to happen. We really made the recession work for us. In 1982 about twelve waterbed stores went out of business in Calgary, including the three that had been well above Terry's at the beginning. But it was our best year. What makes this even more remarkable is that, for the most part, waterbeds don't bring in repeat business. People buy only one waterbed. So we always had to be looking for new markets, even in tough times.

a great time to negotiate

Terry opened a fourth store during that recession, and because the economy was so bad, he was able to negotiate a really good lease. That's one of the biggest lessons I learned from working with Terry: The bottom of the economic cycle is a good time to expand if you are financially solid. I saw the same kind of situation again in my own business a few years later, when I put my offices together in Vancouver around 1985. The market was soft and I was able to get six months of free rent and $25,000 worth of renovations when I moved in—and I didn't even ask for it! They just offered it to me to try to get me in there. If you can afford it, you can really take advantage of that kind of situation. Now in 1992 I'm ready to sign another lease. Yes, another six months of free rent is on the agenda!

Innovative Merchandising

problems in good times

Another person who has implemented many of these winning strategies is Vicki Krotz. Vicki opened a business called Scarboro Fair Fashions in Stratford when the Ontario economy was strong. She was scheduled to open in January 1988, and she had been assured that the store would be ready in time. But when January arrived, it was not. All Vicki's inventory was in her apartment, the bills were coming in, and she had no store. One of the disadvantages of a strong economy is that retail space can be almost impossible to find.

get creative

In a booming economic climate, Vicki was having her own personal recession, which proves that turbulent times are not only associated with a down economy. But Vicki was determined to be successful. She didn't have a store, but what she did have was a large network of friends and relatives in town. She got on the phone and told them all about the predicament she was in. She asked them if they would set up "clothes parties" in their homes that she could come to with her fashions and accessories. From January to August Vicki ran a booming little business selling clothes through parties in private homes.

get out into the community

On August 8 she finally opened a 500-square-foot store. Her months of selling in homes, however, had taught her a few things about how to make the most of her store once she had it. For instance, after Vicki closes at night, you will often see many, many women inside who have booked the store for parties—where groups of friends come to try on clothes, and enjoy themselves. The customers love these parties, and Vicki's business benefits as well.

go the extra mile

Vicki does all kinds of innovative things to boost her business—little things that make a big difference (home deliveries, for example). If a woman phones and wants a pair of running shorts, Vicki just asks the size and then drops by with four or five pairs for the woman to try on. Her business cards are vertical, and she uses them as tags on the clothes, putting the price in the middle. That way, when you take your purchases home, you always have the card, and maybe it will bring you back again.

Vicki also conducts fashion shows on a regular basis for a variety of different groups, which allows her to meet new customers. She and some of her staff are also available to give scarf-tying demonstrations to groups in people's homes. The demonstrations are free, and they provide a golden marketing opportunity. Vicki sold tens of thousands of dollars worth of scarves in 1990 alone.

be green

In addition to all of this, Vicki is on the environmental bandwagon. For every ten bags you bring back, you get a "fashion buck," which is worth a $5 discount. That way, she looks after her best customers and at the same time helps the environment by recycling the bags.

Vicki says—and I think this is really important—that a lot depends on how badly you want something and how far you are willing to go. If things aren't happening for you—in your business or in your life—just make a list of what things you are *not* willing to do in order for something to happen.

Her willingness to make things happen herself earned her the Young Entrepreneur of the Year Award for Southern Ontario in 1990. She now does guest speaking as a hobby, capturing more of the limelight and even new customers! Vicki takes full control of her own economy.

Eight Strategies

Vicki Krotz of Scarboro Fashions and Terry and Corrine Straker of Forty Winks Waterbeds are real-life examples of energetic businesspeople who took positive control of their own economy. You can do it too! Just follow these eight strategies.

1. Never say die! Vicki Krotz didn't. She said to herself, "There has got to be something I can do. There is a way out of this." When The Brick was moving to town, Terry said, "There has to be a way to combat The Brick's grand opening." He found it in the money drop. When facing your own challenges, say to yourself, "There is a way to handle this." Then call on your past experiences, talent, staff, friends, and associates to come up with an answer.
2. Hire the expertise. Terry hired Dennis Webb and me to help him overtake the competitors. Find out who the experts are in the area you need help in. Invest in expertise, but at the same time make it an educational experience. Terry didn't need us after he got rolling. He had learned the necessary skills from us.
3. Know your customers. Put in tracking systems so you know who buys, when they buy, how much they spend, what brings them to you, what keeps them away, and what would persuade them to buy

more often. You have to know these details to control your own economy. Advertising, tracking, and gathering customer information will be explored further in Chapter 10.

4. Implement innovative and outrageous advertising and promotion ideas and concepts. It makes you stand out from the crowd. Vicki was innovative. She conducted scarf-tying demonstrations, opened her store after hours for special functions, and became a popular local speaker. Terry was outrageous with his Mr. Money Drop promotion. Being innovative and outrageous makes you stand out from the crowd, usually at less cost. It is a great way to move the market and take control of your own economy.
5. Think like a commando! Do things that the competition will have trouble detecting and copying right away. Vicki had her clientele built up before she opened the store. Terry launched Mr. Money without The Brick knowing it was coming. The element of surprise gave him an edge. Chapter 6 is all about commando thinking.
6. Buy right. Terry bought the right beds and bedroom furniture at the right price. Chapter 11 will show you ways to buy better so that you have better control of your own economy.
7. Become sales-oriented. Both Terry and Vicki had sales-oriented businesses. Everybody needs to sell in turbulent times. Train everybody in your business to be sales-oriented, not just service-oriented. Chapter 7 presents more information on how to get everyone selling.
8. Service! Service! Service! This is Vicki Krotz! Implement a strategy to improve service. Super service will put you in control of your market. Chapter 9 details how to set up a super service system and how several businesses have benefited from giving customers the royal treatment.

These eight strategies are only the beginning. This entire book is packed with money-making ideas, stories, and how to's that will definitely put you in control of boosting your business in any economy.

Questions to ask yourself:

- What is one situation I need to take control of right now?
- What steps am I going to take to control the situation?
- Which one of the eight strategies presented here could I use to improve my situation?
- Do I have the right experience to improve my situation, or should I hire someone?
- Who could give me a hand?

CHAPTER THREE

Walking on Ceilings

is this book for me?

At this point many of you are thinking about the examples I've given and maybe saying, "Yes, but that's a retail story and it doesn't apply to me because we are in the trucking business." Somebody else might be saying, "Yes, but that's Calgary, Alberta, and I live in Florida. That can't have anything to do with me." Or maybe it's, "Yes, but we are a much larger company." Another one may say, "Yes, but I don't have any money, and that guy in the waterbed business obviously had some money to be able to advertise like that. I can't afford to advertise."

yeah, buts

I call these kinds of thoughts the "yeah, buts." A "yeah, but" person looks at a problem but doesn't look for ways to solve it, to change it, or to make it work. They say, "Yes, but it won't work," and then dismiss it. They lack creativity and vision. My objective is to show you how to overcome the "yeah, buts"—how to take the information in this book and apply it to your business situation.

Business is basic. Everything that Terry and Vicki did was basic and applies to every business, regardless of its size or nature. They didn't use any magic. They did some basic things that created the end results they wanted. Terry discovered that his customers were a useful resource, so he asked them for information. Anybody can do that. Vicki didn't have a store, so she sold with what she did have—a lot of friends and a lot of determination. Everybody has something they can use as a resource; they only have to recognize it.

I knew a plumber in a small prairie town called Lloydminster who had a group of employees who had been with him from fifteen to twenty years. He was badly hit during a downturn in the economy and didn't have enough business to keep them busy. But how do you lay off a man who's worked for you for twenty years? He's your friend; his kids come to your Christmas party.

diversify

So the plumber decided to diversify his business. He looked around the community for a new niche, and in the end created a department for underground sprinkler systems. He put one of the twenty-year employees in charge of developing and marketing an underground sprinkler system for lawns. Then he expanded into the retail business and started promoting do-it-yourself items. Customers could get advice from a fully qualified plumber on how to put a tap in. He put another employee, who had been with him for seventeen years, in charge of the store.

The retail part of the business grew, and they moved one of the other plumbers in, too. The underground sprinkler department blossomed and one of the other plumbers moved in there. When the opportunity came along to bid on a million-dollar plumbing contract, the plumber was in a position to do so. He had a whole nucleus of fully trained, experienced plumbers who he had kept through the economic downturn by diversifying his business and by asking one basic question: "What can I do with my existing resources?" Anybody in any business can do that.

The Importance of Research and Brainstorming

know in advance

It is important to research the competition before launching new business ideas. Sherry's Sweet Shop provides an excellent example of how to use potential customers as a resource. Before she began her business, Sherry stood in front of the main competitor's store with her clipboard and did all kinds of research. She had a whole list of questions—what types of chocolates customers wanted, what specialty services would interest them, whether they would send flowers on Valentine's Day, and so on. She was aware of her competitor's strengths and weaknesses before she even launched her own business.

Digger's Roadhouse provides another example of researching the competition. Barry Gunn, the owner of Digger's, attended one of our owner development programs. During the ten-month program period, he devised a unique way to improve service, increase staff involvement, and evaluate the competition. Once a month, four staff members are asked to select a competitive restaurant from a list and go out to dinner—compliments of Digger's, of course. The next day, before opening, the Digger's staff meets, and the four staff members who had dinner duty report on their night out. The only restriction is that the diners can only report on the good things the competitor is doing. Exceptions are granted only if the staff notices something amiss that Digger's is also doing. Discussion then centers on making a correction to Digger's service.

brainstorming

Employees can make important contributions to brainstorming sessions. Brainstorming involves a group of people contributing ideas and suggestions related to a given topic. The group suggests as many ideas as possible in a given time period without stopping to evaluate the ideas put forward. The process that I suggest is as follows:

- Invite a group of staff members and outsiders (if appropriate) to join you in a brainstorming session about a certain topic.
- At the beginning of the session, review the rules of brainstorming and clarify the objective. Emphasize the importance of *no evaluation* during the free-flow of ideas. Assure everyone that there will be an opportunity to evaluate after the free-flow.
- Use a flip chart and have a volunteer be the official recorder. It is easier to have another person tape each page to the wall once the sheets are complete, or tape blank sheets to the wall in advance.
- Post the topic or question that the group will be focusing on where everyone can see it.
- Start the free-flow process and encourage the group members to contribute their ideas quickly, without evaluating them or anyone else's. Aim for quantity; quality will surface during the process.
- Begin the evaluation at the end of the time period or after you've received sufficient ideas. I often sort ideas into the following categories:

    1. *Excellent* ideas that can be started immediately with a minimal investment.
    2. *Fair* or *good* ideas that may require a substantial amount of money or effort to implement.
    3. *Okay* ideas that you may want to look at in the future.
    4. *Storage* ideas that you would rather put away.

- Reevaluate your excellent ideas and narrow them down to a few that you wish to implement. Set the others aside temporarily.
- Implement the ideas by deciding who, what, when, how, where, and with what. Continually monitor to ensure that you do not try to do too much, too quickly. Each person should have a flow chart or schedule of his or her implementation responsibilities. Set a time for follow-up.
- During the follow-up sessions, be prepared to make adjustments. Very few plans ever go exactly the way we want them to. Good ideas fade without follow-up.

An electrical contractor who also was in one of our ten-month owner development programs sat down and brainstormed with his staff about how to improve customer service. They came up with most of the things you would expect: keep the truck clean; institute a truck replacement policy so they wouldn't have run-down, unreliable vehicles; keep the uniforms clean; and so on. Then one of the guys said, "Hey, we carry our tool boxes around in the back of the truck, and they get pretty dirty. But we often go into pretty nice offices and homes. Why don't we carry a piece of carpet with us to put on the floor, and put the tool box on top of the carpet so the customer's floor stays clean?"

This was a very basic idea—not magic, basic. But basic can work magic sometimes. That electrical contractor got phone calls from all over the city saying, "I have never had such a caring serviceman in my home before. Do you know what he did? He put down a piece of carpet to keep my floor clean. I'm never going to call anybody else but Harris Electric, believe me." A little thing like that developed incredible loyalty.

Making the Most of Your Resources

tap your employees

Whether you sell products or services, good employees are a key resource, and good resources are worth cultivating. If you have a retail store and your best days are Friday night and Saturday, then it's a good investment to get the best employees to work then, even if it costs you more. Often the best employee says, "Hey, I don't want to work Friday night and Saturday." So the store is staffed those days by new people and part-timers who are not as good with customers. So you make an investment. Maybe you pay more per hour. Maybe you say, "I'll tell you what; you can have a whole day off if you give us four hours on Friday night." If you can get your best people to work this way, you can easily make your money back and more.

tap your clients

Customers, employees, or anyone who is part of your business is a potential source of ideas and knowledge. Suppose you are a manufacturer who delivers to a distributor, who then delivers to a retail store, who then sells to the public. You're a long way down the chain from your customers. However, you can sit down with your distributors and find out what they really need to help them sell more of your products to their retail stores. We all have a base of knowledge and ideas that we can draw on no matter what kind of business we are in.

Stu Leonard's grocery and dairy market in Connecticut holds customer focus group meetings every Saturday morning. In one meeting, a customer suggested that they have fresh fish. The supervisor of the fish department stated that their fish comes in fresh from the Boston piers daily. The customer proceeded to say that she meant unpackaged fish. With that suggestion, the store owners put another freezer of unpackaged fish across the aisle from the packaged fish. To their surprise, fish sales doubled. This is an excellent example of the benefit of listening to what your customers have to say.

Make a list of six customers you could invite to a customer focus group. Next, list the situations you'd like to explore with this valuable resource group. Focus groups are great. They allow you to develop relationships and gather information at the same time.

For example, accountants don't go out and knock on doors to get their clients, but they can use existing clients as a resource to generate new ones. A friend of mine had an accountant who ran a series of information seminars for his clients on the general sales tax, telling them to bring a friend. A lot of the friends thought, "Gee, my accountant hasn't given me this kind of useful information," and they switched accountants.

let them try it before they buy

While working on this book, my editor, Greg Ioannou, told me how his own accountant expanded the services he offered to existing clients. He said to Greg, who is a partner in a small publishing-related firm, "You could benefit from some more financial planning. Let me do a plan for you—free. If it's useful to you, we can do it on a regular basis. If not, what have you got to lose?"

give me good surprises

And anyone, even accountants, can find ways to look after customers. We had an accountant in one of our programs in Nanaimo, B.C., who found out from talking to a few customers that many of them were bothered by the lack of free parking in the neighborhood. So the firm started keeping a supply of change at the front desk. Whenever clients called to set up an appointment, they would tell them, "Make sure you drop by and pick up some change from us for the parking meter. No charge." Can you imagine that—an accounting firm giving away money? It was just an extra little thing, and it didn't cost them much. But those little things can make all the difference. What are the exceptional little things you could do for customers or distributors that would leave an impression?

Are you still saying, "Yes, but . . . ." Are you still asking, "How does a little fashion store in Stratford or a waterbed store in B.C. or an accountant in Toronto have anything to do with my Portland, Oregon gravel pit?"

Well, throw a party at the gravel pit. You could have a big picnic and make it such an event that the gravel pit party is *the* place in town to go. Use the event as an opportunity to educate people about your product. What's the price of gravel? What can you use it for, besides roads—flower beds, lanes? What makes good gravel as opposed to bad? If you sell both sand and gravel, what about promoting sandbox sand? One of the hardest things to find is sand for backyard sandboxes.

be outrageous

Suppose your business is dog grooming. Could you hold a dog fashion show? Offer free advice on dog nutrition? Try taking a few really sharp-looking dogs for a walk around a likely neighborhood—maybe a seniors' community. If you want to make sure everyone notices, put your spouse in a dog costume and take him or her for a walk with a sign that says, "Let Us Walk Your Dog." Or adapt Vicki's business card idea: Put little business cards on the bows or collars.

What if you give tuba lessons? You need to find ways to expand that small market. You could give miniconcerts in shopping malls, combined with little lectures or conversations about how the tuba works. You could give out fancy coupons for a first tuba lesson free, or start a brass band at the local community center.

Think Small

If you work for a big company and you are thinking, "Well, gee, these all sound like small businesses, this stuff may not be for me," remember that a big company is just a bunch of little companies put together. Plenty of major companies these days are trying to think like smaller companies; they are trying to find ways to have the flexibility, the creativity, the entrepreneurship, and the innovation that a smaller business can have.

all business is small business

Although a lot of this book is geared toward small businesses, it is not the size of the business that matters as much as how you think about business. And small business thinking is what you are going to have to take into your big corporation to really succeed in the 1990s. Small is effective.

walking on ceilings

I remember reading recently about why flies can walk on ceilings. I am not a scientist and I really don't understand physics, but I know that the law of gravity means that you and I stay on the ground. We can't walk on ceilings. So why is it that a fly can walk on ceilings? They don't have sticky feet. They don't have suction cups or little hooks. It's a law that is stronger than the law of gravity at that size. They stay on ceilings because they are so small that they are attracted to the big object. They don't even know they're on the ceiling.

Small companies are like flies. They can do things that big companies can't. The law of gravity drives the economy, keeping big companies on the ground. When they meet an obstacle—such as a recession—they are stuck. But small companies can walk on ceilings. If, for instance, the waterbed shop has five busy days in the month, it can have two or three times as many staff for those five days. IBM, however, can't triple its staff once a month. At least, the whole of IBM couldn't. But big companies that think in units of small can also walk on ceilings. Little bits of IBM, after all, are just like a bunch of little waterbed companies.

be local

Suppose you are the manager of a branch of a national bank. You might make the mistake of thinking, "I am part of a national organization. They advertise for me. We are part of a national image, and that is what makes me successful." That's nonsense. If you are managing a local branch, your market is a square mile—no different from the local grocery store or the local shoe store. Your clients are the local people, and that's who you go after in that kind of situation. What are their needs? What language do they speak? What day is their payday?

A number of years ago while consulting with The Royal Bank, we put up a sign in the window with eleven languages on it, including Italian, Chinese, Japanese, French, and English. They had people working in the bank who spoke more than one language. In fact, they discovered that they had eleven different languages at their disposal. This branch also started conducting money management seminars and talks for the Royal Canadian Mounted Police located nearby.

You may be fortunate enough to have the backing of a national company and national advertising. But if you're smart, you'll run that business as if it were your own. You make it yours, and market it in the same way, because if you don't you lose out. People will go three blocks down the street to the branch where the manager and the rest of the people running it are a team, marketing over and above the message that says, "We are a big national company."

small is big

Small is big, or big is small. However you want to put it, think small and you'll have a big success. Think innovative. Think creative. Take control of your own economy in your own branch of whatever you do.

Whatever your size, find out who your customers are and what they want, then treat them accordingly. Great marketers are not leaders but followers. They listen carefully to their customers or to the people who work with them, then they provide what the people need.

be alert

Don't be afraid of change. If you are going to ride the waves, you have to let them carry you. Be alert for opportunities all the time. If you see something you like, and if something inside of you says, "Oooh, that sounds good," but another part of you says, "But it wouldn't work for me," disregard the "but it wouldn't work for me." Keep the first thought. Identify what it was that made you feel it was a good idea. Then get together with somebody else and say, "How could we take this and apply it to our business?"

Always look for an element of an idea that you can apply to your business. The idea itself doesn't have to be directly applicable. The key is to learn to take the elements you can use. That way, whenever you hear a success story like Forty Winks Waterbeds or Scarboro Fair Fashions, you can find something in it that will work for you. Don't be a "Yes, but" person. Be a "Do it" person—someone who looks for ways to make it work.

Become like a fly. Walk on ceilings. Even if you are a big business, government, or association, you can operate like a small business. Manufacturers can use a retail idea if they ask themselves, "How does the main idea apply to my business?" We are only limited by our "Yes, buts."

Questions to ask yourself:

- In which areas have I been saying, "Yes, but" too often?
- What actions can I take to change this?
- What problems and/or opportunities can I brainstorm about right now?
- If I work in a large company, how can I operate more like a small business?
- Which two ideas in this chapter can I apply to my own business or life?

CHAPTER
FOUR

Face the Facts

A few years ago, something happened to me that changed my direction from a downswing to an upswing. In the middle of the night, I woke up feeling like I had concrete running from the back of my head to the lower part of my back. Every muscle in my body was tight.

My wife woke up at the same time and said, "You have been tossing and turning, and I can hear you mumbling in your sleep, Bill. I've never seen you this uptight, except for the time when you first opened your business nine or ten years ago. What's going on? You teach stress management, but you're so stressed out. What is it?" I couldn't identify it.

In the morning, I went to my office and started to prepare for a program that our company was putting together. I had asked one of my associates, Jim Reger, to send me an article I had seen in the *Harvard Business Review* in 1983—"The Five Stages of Small Business Growth" by Neil C. Churchill and Virginia L. Lewis. That article happened to be sitting on my desk. I flipped it open and saw a chart that explained the five stages of small business growth.

As I read the chart, I began to feel less stressed. I realized that many of the challenges I was facing were the result of my business's growth. This chart (see Figure 4.1) showed me that I was at a point called "takeoff" in small business growth. A lot of things were happening to me and my business that I didn't understand, but once I read about the takeoff stage, I realized that I wasn't different than any other company owner who was in the same stage. I have been buying reprints of that article in the *Harvard Business Review* for years now and giving them to my clients on consulting assignments.

know where you are, know where you're going

One of the most important factors in making things happen in your life is knowing where you are. A captain was once asked, "What does it take to get to a certain destination?" He said, "I need two things. I need to know what the destination is—say, London, England—and where I am before I start, for example, where on the ocean." These are the two facts that we need to know, and to face, in our business lives: Where are we now? Where do we want to go? If you are involved in the running or owning of

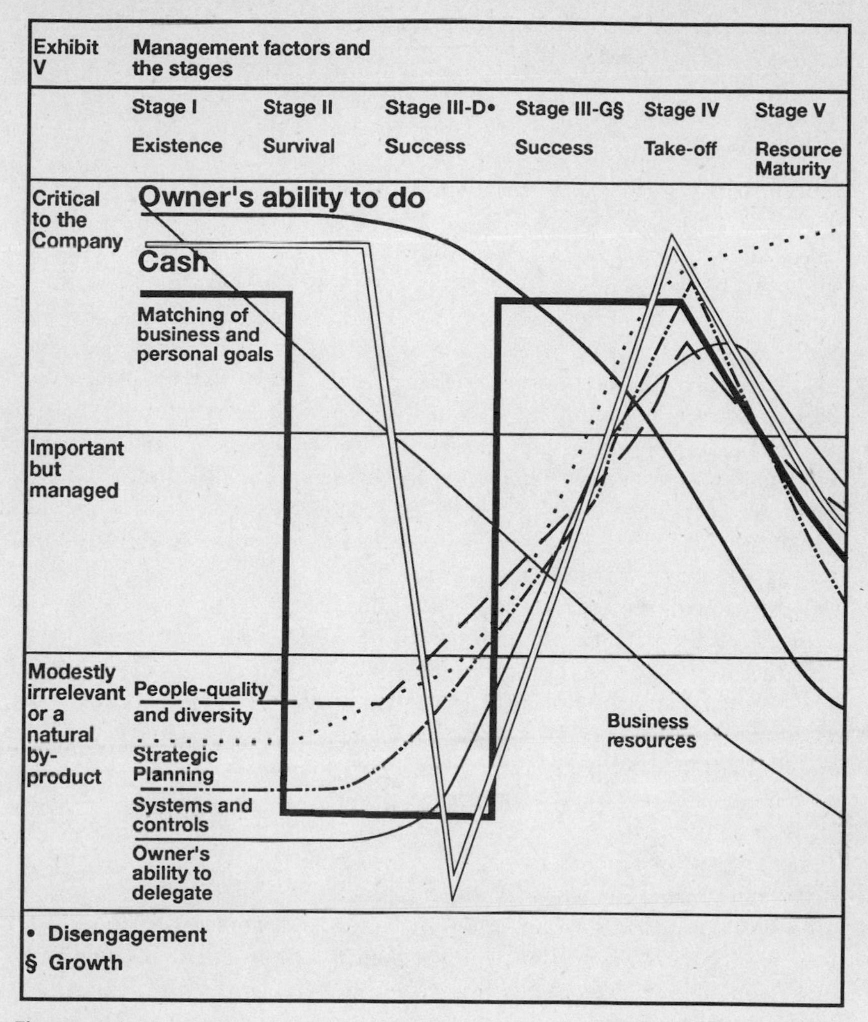

Figure 4.1 Management factors and the stages. (To obtain Neil C. Churchill's and Victoria L. Lewis' original in-depth article titled "Growing Concerns—The Five Stages of Business Growth," contact the *Harvard Business Review* and ask for reprint No. 83301. Neil C. Churchill can be reached at Babson College, Wellesley, Massachusetts.)

a business, or if you plan to be, it is important to know what the five stages of small business growth are.

The Existence Stage

what's important

The first stage is the existence stage. Anyone who has started a business in the last two years is probably at this stage; however, some businesses spend their entire lives there because they just don't have the ability to grow. According to the *Harvard Business Review* article, there are three types of management factors that exist in all five stages: (1) factors that are *critical* to the company, (2) factors that are *important* but managed, and (3) factors that are *modestly irrelevant* or natural by-products. You must assess what is critical, important, and irrelevant and respond accordingly.

work hard

For example, in a new business it is absolutely critical that the owner work hard to make things happen. At the existence stage, you must be prepared to work fifty- to eighty-hour weeks. A successful business requires much time and effort. You have to be willing to learn how to sell and how to call on clients; it's absolutely critical to develop a market niche and to develop enough customers to help the company grow so you can stay in business. Selling is vital at this stage in any kind of business. If you can't sell, then you have to hire somebody who can. You must, however, at least understand what's going on because you're going to have to do everything else to back that person up. You are the company, and you have to work to make things happen.

The quality and the diversity of the people you hire is not as critical an issue in the existence stage because you are doing most of the work. You are directing and telling others what you want them to do. You don't have to go out and hire top-notch, powerhouse people. You just want good people who will do a good job and who will listen and work with you. If you happen to get top-notch people, it is a bonus—not an essential ingredient. Also, your ability to delegate at this stage is not crucial because you are still doing most of the work.

watch your pennies

In the existence stage it is also critical to watch your cash daily, and in some cases hourly. You've got to keep your eye on the cash—how much money is coming in, how much is going out. You can't afford to be loose with it.

stay focused

Another critical factor in the existence stage is being realistic about your business and personal goals. You can't plan on having a lot of recreation time. You do not want to have a goal to build a cabin out at the lake the year you open your business. If you are trying to do that while your business is at the existence stage, the chances of success are very, very low. Stay focused.

Strategic planning is only a modestly relevant factor in the existence stage. As a matter of fact, your strategic plan consists of one thing—to make enough money to be in business tomorrow. If you go much beyond that, you can get caught wasting a lot of time and not making success happen. Spend more time learning how to use the tools of the trade, finding reliable suppliers, and tapping into the proper business resources. These are more critical issues at this stage.

get the resources you need

Setting up complex systems and controls (computer systems and elaborate paperwork) is also irrelevant at this point because, once again, you are doing most of the work yourself. The business is too small, and spending too much effort in that area uses resources better spent on generating sales and delivering the product or service.

sell and deliver

The Survival Stage

If you make it past the existence stage, which hopefully most of us do, you enter the survival stage. The survival stage is much like the existence stage, only here you are making enough money so that it isn't necessary to focus on customers every minute of the day. (However, your focus on the customer is still critical to the company.) Your reputation is beginning to develop, and business is starting to roll in.

things improve

The quality and diversity of your people is still modestly irrelevant in the survival stage, as is the need for much strategic planning. Systems and controls are also minimal because you are still doing most of the work yourself or are telling people what you want them to do.

At this point, you should have enough money coming in to repair equipment, if necessary. If you are in a consulting business, you can now afford to buy a new suit or a new pair of shoes. You might be able to afford to get your car painted. These things tell you that you are doing a bit better and that you have gone beyond the existence stage. You must still work hard, however, to move your business into the next stage—the success stage.

a few more dollars

The Success Stage

The success stage has two substages: Success D, which means Success Disengagement, and Success G, which means Success Growth. Success D occurs when you no longer have to watch your cash flow every day. You can check it on the balance sheet or the financial statements at the end of the month. You are not worried about where the money is coming from because you have a good customer base. The investment that you have made in advertising, positioning, finding your niche, and getting your products accepted is starting to pay off.

Success D Stage

starting to delegate

The owner's workload begins to drop in this stage. What you do is still critical to the company, but you are not responsible for as much as you used to be. As the owner, you begin to delegate more to the staff.

At this point, you do not have to match your business and personal goals. Business is going well enough that someone else can run it. You must still watch fairly closely, but you can go off and do other things. You can start another business venture; you can build that cabin; you can meditate on a mountaintop for a week or two if that's what you want to do. It is not essential that you be involved in every phase of the business as long as you have systems to monitor it and good people to operate it.

At this stage, the strategic planning you do and the systems you set up are important but not critical. It is more important that you hire the right people; people who will do the best job but who will not push the company into the next growth stage—a stage you may not be financially ready to enter or finance. Of course, the continuation of marketing and development of business resources and training remain important.

franchises

Many companies in the Success D stage are franchises. People who buy franchises are usually only able to build them up to a certain point because all of the other franchises have been bought from the franchiser and there is no room left for growth. After everything is working well, the franchisee may decide to get into other business ventures. Franchises often move from existence to Success D much faster than a community business that does not have the support and systems provided by the experienced franchiser. The downside is that if the economic climate changes quickly, the franchisee may not have had enough experience in the first two stages to know what to do under pressure. This places stress on both the franchiser and franchisee.

community business

A Success D type business can also be a community business that either doesn't have the market for growth or that has an owner who has made a conscious decision not to grow. The owner might decide, "I don't want the headaches. I'm happy, and I've got a nice little cash cow going here. Why should I rock the boat?"

Success G

If you decide that you do want to grow, you will enter the Success G stage. (Because many companies end up in the growth stage unintentionally. This often happens by reacting to continual opportunities.) At this stage you have reached the platform for growth. You must begin to assemble your credit and your good people because you are building a foundation that will allow you to take off.

focus on tomorrow

Closer monitoring and managing of your cash flow is more important in the Success G stage than in the Success D stage because more cash is flowing in, and more is flowing out. At this stage you do less of the work yourself and need more qualified people to help. The business is moving faster.

When you are in the Success G stage, you must consider the future in everything you do—from the people you hire, to the equipment you buy, to the marketing materials you put together. You are at a plateau preparing for the takeoff. Your strategic planning should begin to kick in, and you have to work hard to make sure that your plan works. You must plan where you want to go. You must determine your goals and the core values of the organization.

get your plan together

You must also begin to build your systems and controls. For example, you need to establish quality control and proper accounting systems that will immediately give you information to make good business decisions. When you build these systems, be sure they will be able to handle your future needs as well.

setting up systems

At this point you have highly competent people working for you, and you must be prepared to delegate. The business is going to grow at such a fast pace that you won't be able to handle all the situations and challenges yourself. You must trust the people you have hired and understand that things may not always be done quite the way you think they should be, or not as well as you could have done them yourself. However, the systems that you put in place should minimize errors. You may even notice that the business may run better than if you ran it yourself.

trust your people

In the Success G stage there is still a focus on business resources and the niche of business you are after, but you spend more time developing the people you work with. Keeping them supported and motivated is as important as your strategic planning and your systems and controls.

A lot of businesspeople get into a growth stage and then realize that they really don't want to be there. They have other goals in their lives besides work, and they didn't know anything about these stages. They thought growth was kind of neat; they had more people working with them in more impressive surroundings. Then one morning they wake up stressed out because they don't have any time to themselves, the quality of their work is not very good, customers are complaining, and the cash flow is tight. They unknowingly grew into the takeoff or Success G stage. If they want to, they can focus on moving back from the takeoff stage to the Success G or Success D stage or even to a survival stage. It *is* possible to move back to another stage. Sometimes you have no choice.

The Takeoff Stage

In the takeoff stage all factors are critical, especially the quality and diversity of your people. You must have top-notch people—people who know things that you don't even know yourself; people who add value; people who support you; people who will take the lead when you are tired. Your ability to delegate responsibility to them is crucial. Your strategic planning is also

over drive

crucial, and you must continually evaluate your systems. Even though you try to keep up with it, your business is moving so fast that the systems are often a bit behind.

Another danger in the takeoff stage is that it's easy to go beyond your cash flow. Your company is moving very fast. There is a tremendous amount of cash coming in and going out. If you don't watch the cash closely, you can be spending more money than you have coming in because of the cost of your growth. In other words, you have outdistanced your cash flow. Line up your credit or inventory long before you need it. (It should have been done at the Success G stage.) Institutions do not usually give you money when you need it. They give it to you when you look strong.

keep your hands on the wheel

The matching of your business and personal goals is vital in a takeoff stage. There is no time to be going off and building that cabin. You must stay on top of everything. Running a business is like going down the road in an automobile that's going 15 miles an hour: It's easy to turn around and talk to somebody in the back seat, have a really nice conversation, and eventually turn around and keep the car on the road. However, if you're driving 200 miles an hour and you turn around, before you know it you're in a field somewhere. It's the same with a company that's in the takeoff stage: it's going so fast that if you're not at the controls watching very closely, you can be so far off the road that it may be impossible to get back. An article by Flemming Meeks ("Keep Your Eye on the Track," *Fortune*, January 6, 1992) demonstrates what can happen when you're moving fast.

In March of 1991 Charles Morgan Jr., chief executive of Acxiom, Conway, Arkansas, won the 12-hour Nissan Camel Grand Prix in his class with a co-driver, collecting an $18,000 purse. Winning speed: an average of 86.9 mph. It was his second win at Florida's Sebring International Raceway in as many years.

When he compares business with car racing, Morgan is talking about his own insistence on keeping Acxiom focused so as not to become diverted or spread too thin. A lanky Arkansan with an engineering degree from the University of Arkansas, Morgan decided to focus exclusively on the direct marketing industry. To generate business, he began courting mailing list brokers, touting the company's data processing prowess. By 1983 revenues of what was then known as CCX Network had grown to $7.5 million. Little Rock-based Stephens Inc. sold 20 percent of the company to the public, at a split-adjusted price of $8, raising $4.3 million.

Then Morgan took his eyes off the track to gaze at the scenery. Using stock, and cash from a $6.5 million secondary offering, he made acquisitions in related but separate fields. He scooped up a mailing house, a software firm specializing in catalogers, and two British data processing firms specializing in marketing. The idea was to turn the company into a one-stop shop for direct marketers.

It didn't work. Not only did some of the acquisitions not work out, but they also diverted Morgan's attention from his core business. The mail shop—at best a low-margin business—has yet to produce the expected synergy with the data processing business. Citicorp, for example, still uses a competitor to handle its mailings. American Express gives its mailing business to Acxiom but runs its own elaborate marketing databases. The catalog fulfillment business was discontinued last year after Acxiom sank over $6 million into buildings and equipment. And the British operations will lose several million dollars in fiscal 1992.

Meanwhile, growth in the core business has stalled in the recession. For example, Chase Manhattan Bank, which paid Acxiom about $6 million for credit card work in 1990, cut its business more than 50 percent in 1991.

Morgan quickly refocused his attention. In early 1991 he cut Acxiom's work force by 7 percent and pared back the executive staff from 34 to 24, taking a 46 percent salary cut himself, to $209,000, and trimming his racing schedule from 15 events in 1990 to just 9 in 1991. The time thus saved he is devoting to working with Acxiom's research and development department to stay close to the technical needs of customers. Over the Thanksgiving holiday he finished writing a key piece of software that simplifies customer access, over dedicated phone lines, to Acxiom's mainframes in Conway.

In order to expand without diverting too much attention from the basic business, Morgan is turning to joint ventures. Long-term deals with the nation's biggest junk mailer, Advo, as well as with Fulfillment Corp. of America, a magazine service firm, among others, should make up for lost computer processing revenues. Morgan says that several similar deals are in the works.

All in all, things are looking better. Dathan Gaskill, an analyst at Stephens Inc., thinks Acxiom's earnings should recover to $1.20 in fiscal 1993, although he readily concedes that Congress or the economy could delay the comeback.

Being the winning driver that he is, Charles Morgan will no doubt keep his eyes on the business road in the future—at the speed he likes to travel, both in business and on the race track. In takeoff you don't relax your eyes for a second. If you do, you better have a codriver!

The first attempt at the takeoff stage often fails. The danger of the takeoff stage is that some people start to believe that they are all-powerful and that they can finance anything. That's what usually kills entrepreneurs. Business gets beyond them. They believe they can do everything, but they can't. They have to delegate. They really have to get their goals and their vision straight, have the right people in place, and have all their systems laid out and the necessary financing for growth in place.

The Resource Maturity Stage

You have successfully made it through the hectic takeoff stage and have hit the resource maturity stage. Now you have all the right people on board, your systems and controls are in place and are solid, top-notch executives are running your business, and your own workload is an irrelevant factor. You could pull away and do other things. In fact, you could actually disengage with a lot more money and a much better income and position.

watch out for apathy

Your strategic planning is absolutely critical to the company during the resource maturity stage, so you must continue to keep your business plans together and follow them closely. Although the clients are rolling in, you still must keep a close eye on the market because there is always a danger that business might change or that new competitors might emerge. If you are not alert, these things can cause some problems. Company shareholders or directors often oust company founders who are not alert to changes in the business climate or who are unwilling to change. Such founders get caught in believing they know all and are all powerful. However, they must be willing to adapt to change if they hope to be around for the resource maturity years. You must ask yourself, "Am I willing to change? Am I holding on to old ideas while everything else is going in another direction?"

stay entrepreneurial

You should have a research and development department to keep up with any changes in the market. Start spinning your company off and making new departments that will stay innovative and entrepreneurial to keep up with the changing markets. Begin holding business opportunities meetings to help you stay innovative. Reward your people for taking some risks. Use these strategies to become a large business with small business capabilities, not a giant that's impossible to turn around.

Assessing Where You Are and Moving to the Next Stage

By now you should know which stage of growth your company is in. I have taught sessions in which people in the audience owned small businesses that had been in the existence stage for five years. After they learned what stage they were in, they became a bit depressed and asked, "My gosh, is this my future? Is this the rest of my life? I thought there was some hope it would get better than this." If this is how you are feeling, you have to stop and put things into perspective.

put it in perspective

Think about the person you used to work for before you started your business. Think about how upset you sometimes became because he or she had such control over you. Isn't owning your own business better than that? Realize that you have purchased a job. You own what you could call a "life-style business." It provides a life-style in which everything is *your* choice. If you want to shut it down next week, you can shut it down. If you want to run it for ten years, then you can run it for ten years. But if you find it depressing and you want to go beyond it, then you have to go back to asking yourself, "What is it I am unwilling to do?" That is probably what is holding you back.

I knew a woman who owned a business that had been at the existence stage for about three or four years. She had been conducting strategic planning for a long time. She had all the computers and all the systems set up for when her business became successful, and she had even hired some staff that she could delegate to. But do you know what she was refusing to do? Sell. She was unwilling to make a call to put some marketing together. She was refusing to do the work that would take her to the next stage.

learn to sell or hire someone

Selling is very, very important, as my friend Rick Gibson-Shaw can attest. In 1982 Rick owned a business that was heavily leveraged. He decided to liquidate the business because he could see that it wasn't going to last. Looking back on it shortly thereafter, he found that his strategic weakness was that he didn't know how to sell. He was skilled in production and ran an audiovisual production house, but no one had ever taught him to sell. After realizing this, he said to himself, "I am going to go on straight commission and start to sell on the street in Toronto. I'll learn how to sell or I'll starve." Rick took a sales job and realized that if he had taken the time to go out and sell he would never have had to close down.

Take a lesson from Rick. Don't wait to find your weakness. Realize what you are unwilling to do and then do it. Are you marketing? Are you really prepared to put in the extra hours? Are you pulling on the talent that's available to you to get yourself out of the existence stage? Are you being honest with yourself?

cash up front helps cash flow

You must be creative and use all of your resources to get out of the existence stage. For example, I cowrote a publication called *Exploring Business Opportunites* for the B.C. government with my friend, Dr. Dale Rusnell. Right at the beginning, I said, "We have to have 50 percent of our money up front." Dale had dealt for years with federal and provincial contracts, and yet he had never asked for advanced payment before. He asked me, "How do we get it?" The answer was simple: "We tell them that we need some money up front because we are in a specialized business." If you ask a tailor to make you a suit, you have to give him or her a deposit. Like the tailor, we could ask for a working deposit. Once you start asking, you'll be surprised at how many people are willing to give it to you. There may be some people who will pay you in full, and there may be others with whom you have to strike a deal. Regardless of how you go about it, the important thing is that you go out there, make the sales call, and get some money up front.

focus, focus, focus

Cash is critical at the existence and survival stages, so you must look down all avenues to obtain it. Always strive to generate cash and save on expenses at these two stages, but don't be afraid to spend money to make money. Recent data indicates that a 2 percent higher retention of customers is equal to cutting costs by 10 percent.

a branch manager is like a small business owner

Sometimes a large company can be in various stages at the same time. The total organization may be in the takeoff or resource maturity stage, but a branch that just opened in Flint, Michigan, for example, is in the existence stage. The branch has the systems and capital of the mother company, so it should move through the existence and survival stages quickly. However, if the branch manager doesn't work hard and doesn't watch the cash on a daily basis, it may be tough for the branch to move to the success stage.

Quality control is another problem for many companies. For example, if a company in the growth stage goes from just three or four employees to fourteen or fifteen, it will be more difficult to monitor the work of the staff. It may be necessary to set up a quick system in which someone from the office keeps track of each project and follows up each meeting with a phone call to ask questions about how things are going.

Using Information on Stages and Critical Factors

There are different ways that you can apply this information on stages and critical factors and use it to make money. However, you have to know what stage your company is in, what stage your present or potential customers are in, and how you can best tailor your product or service to their needs. Let's deal with a few hypothetical examples.

what stage are your suppliers at?

As middle management at IBM you are responsible for purchasing and dealing with suppliers. First you must make sure that you are dealing with suppliers you can really count on. There is nothing worse than depending on getting material for certain equipment only to find out that the supplier can't provide what you need. Look at what growth stage the suppliers are in themselves. I would think that IBM probably deals mainly with resource maturity-type companies that can be counted on to deliver and does not deal with new businesses that have just entered the takeoff stage. However, if the established company has become staid, which a lot of them do, and is no longer dependable, innovative, and flexible, then you, as the IBM manager, would want to use a financially sound, innovative, well-organized organization still in the takeoff or Success D stage.

managing a take off department

Suppose you own a middle-sized company that has inadvertently moved into the takeoff stage, and you don't want to be there. How do you move out of it? One way is to prepare to sell your company while business is good. To do this, first put a limit on the length of time it is going to take to back out. Run your business effectively, keeping in mind that you are backing out. For example, if I were going to sell my company, I would set a twelve-month limit for myself because my seminar programs run eight or ten months in length. If I needed the cash flow, it might take ten more programs to make sure that the company was solid, financially. Then I would run my ten best programs with my ten best employees.

Another way to move out of the takeoff stage would be to move my business back into the success stage, where it would run itself. This can't be done overnight. I would have to select my most profitable areas—the market positions where I am really strong—and then I would have to stop spending money on growth. The danger of growth is that it can look like you are making profits; however, in most cases, you are spending the profits for growth purposes. Be sure to forecast accurate costs when moving backward to another stage. You may have to carry the systems and some people just to administer the change.

consciously moving backwards

Another alternative is to subcontract. You may be growing so fast that you are not able to back off. In this case, you should look for people who are aggressive, energetic, and are willing to subcontract some of the business from you.

Your knowledge of the five stages can also be used as a sales and marketing tool. By knowing the different stages that a business could be in, you will be better able to target specific businesses and match your products and/or services to their growth needs.

using the model to sell

For example, let's say that you are an account executive for Management Recruiters International, the largest management and executive recruiting firm in the United States. Because you are placing highly paid executives, you will want to deal with companies that are in the success, takeoff, and resource maturity stages. When talking with Success D owners, you would stress the importance of having a good executive in place to run the business for them so that they can disengage and get on with some of the other things in their lives. If you are dealing with a Success G organization, you would present executives who are of the same caliber as the owner or senior executives you are selling to—someone who could carry some of the load and spearhead parts of the growth. When working with organizations in the maturity stage, you would present executives who had experience in large companies and could keep the company solid.

be careful

Let's examine another example where information about the five stages of business would be valuable as a marketing tool. If you are selling heavy equipment or assembly line equipment, for instance, your biggest potential markets are businesses in the takeoff stage. It's exciting to work with companies that are in the takeoff stage, but you have to watch them almost daily, just like they have to watch their cash flow daily. You have to be careful with your credit and collections. You don't have to watch the Success D or resource maturity-stage businesses as closely because they are not risking as much as the takeoff and growth companies. You have to learn to put flags on certain clients and accounts. It doesn't mean stay away from them. It means keep your eyes open. Don't let the media hype about their success overshadow their credit balance.

Understand these Stages

To make the stages of business growth easier to understand, the key components of each stage are summarized here.

Stage 1: Existence

- Focus on gaining customers.
- Watch your cash flow closely and know your daily break-even point.
- Concentrate on delivering your product and services so that customers will return. The goal is to stabilize quality, delivery, and service.
- Expand your customer, product, and service base so you can grow to the next stage.
- Create a "stay alive" strategy. (In other words, your strategic plan is to be open tomorrow.) There is minimal formal planning.
- As the owner or key executive, become the key source of energy and vision.

  Many businesses don't get beyond this stage. Those that don't make it to Stage 2 usually close down or are sold. Many life-style businesses stay at this stage (for example, an individual carpentry contractor).

Stage 2: Survival

- You should have a small number of employees.
- There should only be one or two levels of management.
- There should be minimal development of systems or formal planning.
- You should have enough money to replace or repair some of your capital assets.
- Start making the business viable and ready for the next stage.
- Don't spend too much capital. You need to save it to finance the growth.
- Know your costs and get the proper margins going. You need to ensure economic returns on labor and equipment costs.
- Since survival is still the main goal, three possible paths you can take are:
  1. Growing in size through profitability.
  2. Remaining the same size.
  3. Going out of business.

Stage 3: Success D (Disengage)

- You should have established good market penetration.
- The owner should be earning average or above average income.
- Staff should have limited upward mobility. (The company isn't growing.)
- First professional staff should be on, such as controller, production scheduler, and so on.
- The basic financial, marketing, and production systems should be in place.
- You may require functional managers.
- Maintain market niche and competitive edge.
- Accumulate sufficient cash for future rough times. (They will come.)
- Reduce direct involvement. (In other words, the owner can disengage more often.)
- Stay alert. Adapt and change. Don't let apathy set in. If you don't stay alert, you may go back to the survival stage or even out of business.

Stage 4: Success G (Growth)

- Expansion should begin.
- Don't outrun your cash flow.
- Develop your staff to meet the needs of a growing company. Keep your eye on the future, not the past.
- Hire qualified executives and managers to help you grow.
- Develop your systems.
- Develop an operational plan.
- Create a strategic plan.
- Reallocate resources (human and capital). You need a line of credit or financing for growth.
- Be prepared to risk all for growth.

If the company is successful, it moves into the takeoff stage. If it isn't successful, the company will move back into the survival stage and then back into Success D, or it will go out of business.

Stage 5: Takeoff

- Ask yourself, "How can I achieve rapid growth and finance that growth?"
- Maintain strong control of your cash to control the growth.

- Deal with the new financial demands and put proper management resources in place.
- If the risk of running the company is too big, it may be time to sell.
- Continually refine systems to deal with growth.
- Delegate responsibilities. Give authority to key managers, for example.
- Beware of sudden economic downswings (loss of market) which can cripple a company at this stage.

Stage 6: Resource Maturity

- Focus more on financial control rather than pushing for larger profits.
- Stay flexible and alert. Respond to change. If there is economic change, new market demands, or new aggressive competitors coming on the scene and you've been taking it easy, you may get knocked back into the survival stage. (Remember, a company with 500 employees and $300 million in sales per year is still a small company. It should be much more flexible than a large company such as General Motors, IBM, or AT&T.)
- Keep the entrepreneurial spirit alive. Let the administrators handle important aspects of the company, but don't let them destroy entrepreneurship and innovation.
- Integrate departments and use performance appraisals.
- Make use of cost controls.
- Staff the company well.
- Implement budgets and strategic planning tools to steer the company.
- You and the business can become quite separate.

Now that you know what stage your company or organization is in right now, you can face the facts about what you've been doing, what you should have been doing, and how and what you will do right now. The facts make business much clearer.

Questions to ask yourself:

- What stage of the small business growth cycle am I in?
- What are the important aspects of operating the business at this stage?
- What am I unwilling to do? How does this affect my business?
- What stage of growth are my existing or potential clients in?
- What opportunities or cautions should I be aware of with my clients?

CHAPTER
FIVE

The Thirty-Minute Snapshot

Have you ever heard yourself say, "I just can't believe it?" It might be about a bad financial situation or a problem employee: "I have told him once, twice, three, four, five times how to do it, and he blew it again. I just can't believe it." Believe it! He did blow it once, twice, three, four, five times. He can't do it. He doesn't have the ability. He doesn't want to do it. He isn't capable, isn't motivated, or something.

One of the biggest problems we have is not believing things that are staring us in the face. If it walks like a duck, and talks like a duck, it is not an eagle—it's a duck.

look at the real picture

Believe a problem exists, and then deal with it. As long as you believe there is no real problem, you won't do anything about solving it. You'll sweep it under the carpet, and your inaction may end up costing you a business and a job. Once you see the problem for what it really is, you are ready to say, "What am I going to do about it?" Once you have looked at the real picture of you and your business, it is much easier to move forward.

supporting attributes

In order to analyze any business situation quickly and simply, I created the thirty-minute snapshot. I devised this snapshot by first asking myself how effective Newport was at that time in terms of staff morale, productivity, sales, financial issues, administration, and advertising (all phases of the business). I determined that we were 70 percent effective. I wrote "70 percent" at the point where 70 percent would appear on the page, then drew a line down the page. I then listed and underlined the various supporting attributes that helped the line reach 70 percent. The stronger attributes received longer underlines than the weaker ones.

opposing attributes

With all these great supporting attributes, it may be difficult for you to understand why that line was not higher up on the page than 70 percent. The reason is that there were opposing attributes pushing in the opposite direction. As a matter of fact, even if I improved many of those supporting attributes, the line may not have moved—it may have just gotten more pressure on it from the opposing attributes. The next step was for me to identify and act on the opposing attributes.

Dealing with Your Opposing Attributes

After I identified the opposing attributes, my objective was to reduce their strength, eliminate them, or turn them into supporting attributes. I brainstormed ideas and methods that could help me achieve one of these objectives with each of the opposing attributes. It is important to note that there will always be opposing attributes that you cannot change. You may have to change the way you think about them if they frustrate you. For example, I cannot change the geography of Canada to reduce my travel and marketing costs, but I might be able to be more effective in my travel schedule.

Once you have put a plan of action together for reducing your opposing attributes, you must examine your supporting attributes to see how you can accentuate them. Once you have done this you have faced reality and are moving toward positive action.

Using the Snapshot to Improve

The overall picture of your business that the snapshot can provide makes a lot of people feel good; they often find that they are better off than they thought. When I do this exercise in my seminars with groups of forty or fifty businesses, I make a master chart of all the supporting and opposing attributes from everyone's company, and people realize that most companies are very similar. Businesspeople find out that they are not alone.

use snapshot and stages of small business growth together

The snapshot can be used in many ways. For example, after looking at the snapshot I put together a number of years ago for my business, Newport Marketing and Communications Inc. (shown in Figure 5.1), I was able to clearly see what my opposing attributes were; I didn't have a strong enough executive team. (I was a one-man executive team.) I didn't have enough time for strategic planning and my systems were strained. The snapshot showed me that I was in the Success G stage of business and enabled me to see what was needed to succeed in the growth and takeoff stages. I immediately put a plan of action together. I hired two key executives, set up qualified regional partners, and purchased expertise and equipment to handle the financial systems. I also held several planning retreats.

You can take any aspect of your business and do a snapshot. You can say, for example, "How good are we in our sales department? What are our supporting and opposing attributes?" Or you can be even more specific: "What's our financial control like around here?" or "What's our advertising like? Supporting attributes? Opposing attributes?" or "What's the motivation

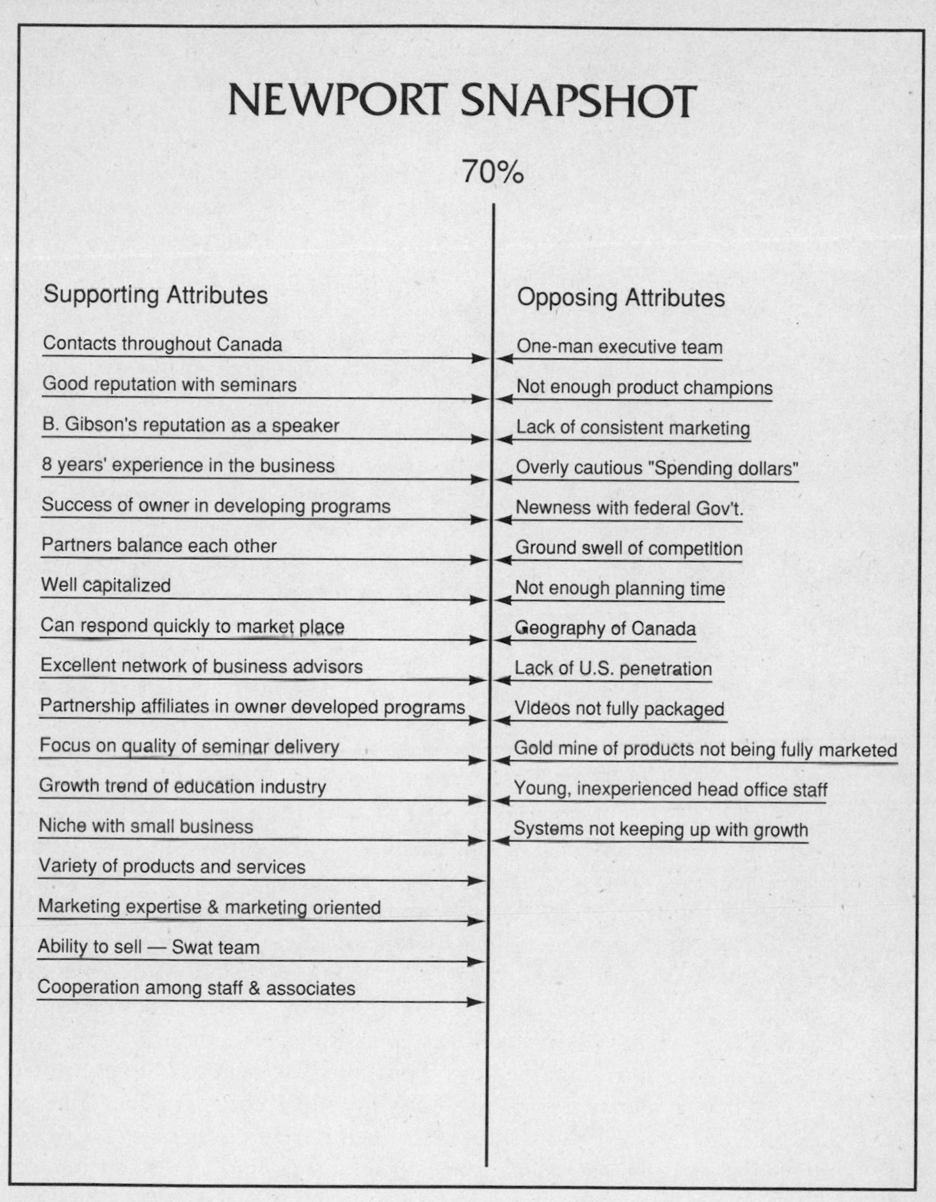

Figure 5.1 Newport snapshot.

of our people like?" You can break it down to a single employee problem: "How effectively are we dealing with this person? Supporting attributes? Opposing attributes?"

personal snapshots

You can also use the snapshot method to determine how effective you are personally in your position in business. I often ask the staff to do this with me, and we discuss the results together. It's a great way to do a staff evaluation. The people who operate or work in the business are the ones who truly make it successful. If the company or department is having problems, it also has something to do with the people who are operating the business. Use the snapshot to help solve these problems.

The snapshot method can also be used as a sales tool. For example, one of my associates would list all the attributes and benefits of his service in front of the customers. Then he would turn the paper over and ask the customers to list the things they weren't pleased with. The customers could usually list no more than three reasons. So they would be holding a long list of supporting reasons to buy and a short list of opposing reasons not to buy.

I have also used the snapshot with communities. This is my favorite way of assessing the economic potential of a community. I was in a small community recently and did this exercise with a group of business leaders. It took about thirty minutes, and now I know the community better than a lot of people who live there. It's a great tool! Use it!

Face the Facts

Paul Hawken, author of *Growing a Business*, tells a story about how Gordon Sherman, the founder of Midas Mufflers, recruited a group of "garage mechanics, wrecking yard owners, and parts dealers" into a group of muffler specialists. Business boomed. His franchisees were bound by agreement to sell only mufflers; however, many were bootlegging shock absorbers—an easy add-on to a muffler once the car was up on the lift. They were easy to diagnose and easy to install. Many franchisees, even those who were his friends, were hiding the shock absorbers from Sherman during inspection.

Although Sherman opposed selling the shock absorbers, he could not do so too forcefully or he could open himself up to antitrust suits. He waged trench warfare on the dealers. They stood their ground and were willing to risk very profitable franchises in order to sell shocks. Sherman could not control the situation.

One morning he decided to face the facts that his dealers knew more than he did. On a closed-circuit broadcast to all the dealers, he announced that Midas Mufflers would be adding shock absorbers immediately to its line. He also initiated a shock absorber sales contest with a trip to the Bahamas as a first prize.

A few years later one of the franchisees invented a machine that allowed him to bend straight tubing into any of the several hundred different shapes required by a fully stocked dealer. The franchisee incorporated a company to market the machine. The franchise agreement was threatened again. The machine could have wiped Sherman out because he was selling his franchisees finished mufflers and tailpipes. Sherman immediately bought the company and asked every dealer who could afford to buy one of the machines to do so. He faced the facts again.

Recently, I went through a similar experience when shifting my personal focus away from operating Newport's Business Owner Development programs throughout Canada. I had several aggressive entrepreneurial associates operating in the various regions. I offered some of them the right to use the Newport name and to continue with the government-funded programs and the nonexclusive use of my materials. For the investment I had in the regions, I wanted a fair sum of money from these people. The reality was that these people now knew all the contacts and how to run the programs. They could succeed without me but would rather have an associate relationship with me—but not at the price I wanted. I faced the facts, took less, received a small royalty on the programs and am now doing new joint ventures. I could have gotten sidetracked and destroyed relationships and potential future business by being unrealistic and not facing the facts.

Peter Thomas, the founder of Century 21 Canada, is the entrepeneur's entrepeneur. His book, *Never Fight With a Pig,* is highly recommended reading. In it he stresses the importance of being realistic.

> *You have to learn how to travel the path of the entrepreneur and win the spoils of battle without becoming stressed out and without losing objectivity because of an oversized competitive ego. The truth is simple—never fight with a pig—never allow yourself to lose sight of your goals and become involved in needless conflicts or hassles that provoke you. If winning will only help you "get even" or "show them who is right" and the victory comes at all costs, it isn't worth it.*

The pig doesn't necessarily refer to an individual; it can mean a situation. Some types of situations or conflicts guarantee that you will get dirty. If you fight with a pig, you can't win. You get dirty, and the pig loves it.

Now that you've had lots of examples to look at, do a snapshot on your department or business, and then do one on yourself, if you haven't already done so. When analyzing your thirty-minute snapshot, don't ignore the realities. Remember that things do not always operate the way you want them to. See them as they are—not the way you wish they would be—and then act.

Questions to ask yourself:

- What are the opposing/supporting attributes of my business?
- What can I do to eliminate, reduce, or reverse each opposing attribute?
- Which supporting attributes can I make stronger?
- How will I achieve the implementation of the above goals?
- Can I use the snapshot method for any other aspects of my business? Which ones?

CHAPTER
SIX

Commando Thinking

One morning, after I spoke at a business owner development program in Red Deer, Alberta, the business advisor who was responsible for the program asked me if I would go on an on-site visit with him to see how we would help a client implement some of the materials. The client owned a Lucky Dollar store. (A Lucky Dollar store is a food store that is slightly larger than a convenience store but smaller than a supermarket.) I asked the owner, "What's one of the toughest things that you are up against? I have about an hour to spend here; what could I do for you in an hour that would really make you happy?"

He said, "Well, Bill, I have about 450 customers come through here on a daily basis, which is a pretty good flow of customers. But they are only spending an average of about $8.50 each. I would really like the average to be higher. Can you give me some ideas on how to do that?"

it could be in front of your eyes

I said, "It's quite simple. The answer is on page 53 of the *Marketing from the Inside Out* book that I gave you on the first evening of the ten-month session. Have you read it?" "I was just getting around to reading it," he said.

Well, on page 53 of that book there was a suggestion for how to increase add-on sales. In the book I used the example of a building supply store where the employees didn't feel comfortable asking for more business while they were making a sale. So we developed a system of checklists. A customer selected an item, and before the clerk went to get it, he or she would hand the customer a clipboard with a checklist on it. For example, if the customer was buying a door, the clipboard would be entitled "Doors" and would have a list below the title that read, "door bells, door knobs, hinges, lights, locks, door mats," etc. The clerk would say, "Just check over this little clipboard here to make sure that you have everything you need. There's nothing worse than arriving home and finding that you forgot something." Then the clerk would leave, get the door, come back, and check the clipboard. In most cases the customer would buy hinges or knobs, and the average sale increased. It was a service to the customer because they didn't feel pressured.

I retold that story to the owner of the Lucky Dollar store who hadn't read the book. Then I said, "Now let's take the same idea and see what we can do for you."

shopping list posters

The key is not to take ideas literally. Use them; change them to fit your business, and make them better. We spent an hour working with that concept. We walked around the store and found ten locations where there was a blank wall about a foot and a half by three feet. I said, "There are ten spots in this store that you are not using. Let's use them. Let's put up ten posters that say 'Shopping List,' and then underneath the title we could write, 'We don't want you to forget anything.' Then under that we could list maybe forty or so items that people might forget when they are shopping, but really need."

The owner started to list items such as bread, milk, and butter, but I suggested that that wasn't really the best move because the markup on bread, butter, or milk is not very high. I suggested putting items on the top part of the poster that give a really nice markup, such as light bulbs. How often do people run out of light bulbs in the home and find that they don't have any? And a light bulb has a good markup on it. So do razor blades, pantyhose, and so on.

So we listed a whole lot of convenience items and put together a chart. But we didn't stop there. I said, "Now what can we do to improve that?" We came up with a little holder on the front of the poster that says, "Take one," with copies of the poster in it reduced to maybe six inches. People could pick up one of these miniature posters, check the items they want, make a couple of notes on it, and take it with them. In addition, we could put out a little container with pencils so that customers could mark the items they were looking for or the ones they had bought. The store owner was slightly concerned that people might take the pencils home and that he might have to spend a lot of money replacing them. So we got really creative and thought to put the store name on the pencils; that way, if people did take them home, at least he would get some advertising out of it. We also thought about leaving a little container by the cash register that said, "Please drop your pencils here" so people could give them back on the way out.

Well, he became very excited about these simple but potentially powerful ideas. The owner kept coming up with new angles, such as throwing a shopping list in the bag for everybody when they are leaving or printing it right on the side of the shopping bags.

The day that all of those little signs went up in that business, the average sale increased dramatically.

Adding to Your Business

The Lucky Dollar store example illustrates commando thinking. Look around and ask, "What are the things that I can do for very little cost to maximize the opportunities in my business?" The competition would never know that you were doing those kinds of things. It's not in the advertising. It's in the store. It's part of the way you do business. The more of this creative marketing that a business uses, the more effective it becomes.

Strategies to get add-ons are very important. We miss a lot of add-on opportunities in our businesses. When your salespeople make calls, even very senior people who have been in the business for twenty-five years, do they really review with the clients all their needs on each visit? Do they have checklists to make sure that they have covered everything? Whether business is slow or strong, we must maximize every opportunity for customer contact. Too often we don't do it.

The same principle applies in a restaurant. When somebody comes by and says, "Would you like a dessert?" I often say no. But if they come by with a tray and put that dessert in front of my nose so I smell the chocolate cake and pecan pie, chances are I'll probably look around, make sure nobody is watching, and say "Two, please!"

Recently I spent a couple of hours with an automobile dealer who was in one of our programs. This is an experienced automobile dealer who has consultants come in on a regular basis from the United States to work with the salespeople. He wanted to broaden his marketing strategies so that sales skills weren't the only thing the company had going for it. He wanted people to think of them first when buying a car—to create a stronger awareness of the company.

We did a brainstorming exercise. In one round of commando thinking, we came up with the idea of offering coffee and doughnuts to the customers. It was a courtesy. When people came into the showroom the first thing a salesperson would say was not, "Are you looking for a car?" but, "Good morning, could we offer you coffee or a doughnut today?" The staff took up the idea; they were very courteous people. It worked well as a way to break the ice in the showroom.

if it's good, take it to the streets

Later we took the idea even further. "Why stick to the showroom?" I said. "Why don't you select one or two businesses in the community every week—maybe the workplace of somebody who has recently bought from you—and show that you really appreciate the business. One Monday morning, send a couple of people—salespeople or management people—down to the company and say, 'Hey, it's coffee time, and today it's on us. We want to get to know everybody in town, and we just want to show you that we appreciate all the business here in the community.' If you want to use this idea in your business, it is probably best to call ahead to set up the coffee and doughnut session. Leave your business cards but sell nothing. Just treat people well. Setting up a strategy of selecting one business per week can make a major impact in a year.

Imagine the impact of doing that kind of thing for a year in a community. If somebody calls ahead and then walks into your office and brings you a doughnut and coffee, it's pretty hard to feel negative about it. The goodwill will mushroom. That is the result of commando thinking. What we are doing is developing relationships, which develops trust, and eventually turns into business or positive word of mouth.

Improving Sales Meetings

Another commando idea that came out of that auto dealership was a way to enhance staff meetings. The most important thing about a meeting is that everyone walks away feeling that something valuable has come out of it. If people feel it was a waste of time they won't want to do it again.

The auto dealership staff wanted to know how to make their meetings really interesting. I told them about CJCH Radio/C100 FM in Halifax, where I had worked as a salesperson. I gave Chuck Langdon, the sales manager, a hard time once about his meetings, and he got a little upset at me. He said, "Gibson, if you're so bright, why don't *you* run the meeting?" I said I would be glad to. So he said, "Fine. You're on next week."

rotate meeting responsibility

At first, this wasn't a friendly challenge. But the meeting I led went well, and we sat down and discussed it afterward. We both realized that this could be a breakthrough. If we got a salesperson to run the meeting every other week so that sales managers didn't have to do it all the time, maybe we could benefit from the change—more creativity, more interest, and so on. Eventually we started inviting outside businesspeople to come and speak. Someone we all respected from another company in town would come in and talk to us at the meeting to get us motivated. It really made a difference.

go off topic

When I told the car dealership salespeople about this, they said, "Why not take the initiative the other way? Why don't we, as a respected business in town, offer to other companies in the community to go out and speak at their sales and staff meetings and motivate *them*?" This was great commando thinking. Automobile dealerships in smaller communities often have the best resource of training tapes, videos, and so on. They can create a lot of goodwill by offering to share them and talking to businesses about how they operate. The topic doesn't have to be selling. Maybe the top mechanic could go into a sales department and show the salespeople how to make their cars last and get better mileage out of them. It would liven up the meeting, provide a useful service, and promote your company. Commando thinking is more than just being ahead of the competition; it means taking an entirely different (proactive) approach.

Building Relationships

My philosophy is that time is the key to all relationships. If you are willing to spend some time with someone, and if you add to that some sincere assistance, that will equal trust. Trust creates a relationship of one degree or another, which then equals a commitment from both parties. It happens automatically. Once you treat people in a caring way, it makes a difference. When somebody walks into a business with coffee and doughnuts and sits down to talk, the human element kicks in. People become friendly; there's a warmth, and everybody walks away happier.

be real

When you go to a sales meeting and help liven it up by showing people how to look after their cars, and you see them getting excited and writing down ideas, you walk away feeling like you really did something. It makes you feel good. On the other side, they walk away more committed to you and happy that you have been there. So it is real. We are talking about something that goes a little bit deeper than just the idea of marketing and sales.

they don't have to buy

Long-term thinking is important as well. My friend Rick bought a car a little over two years ago, and twice now he has received a phone call from a dealer who did not sell him the car, wishing him a happy birthday. The salesperson keeps track of people's birthdays, and even though Rick didn't buy a car from her—he just talked to her about buying a car—she calls him every year. Next time he needs to buy a car, you can bet he is going to go and see her.

Joseph Citerilla, a businessman from California, took only seven years to build a general insurance agency into a firm that grosses several million dollars a year. Whenever he made bids and didn't get the contracts, he put the people on the list just as though they were customers. When he sent renewal notices out to customers sixty days before renewal time, he would send these people a notice, too. He even put them on the mailing list at Christmas time. He followed up to see how happy they were with their insurance. When the renewal notice hit, many of them called to buy. That's commando thinking! (This is similar to what Terry and Corrine Straker did at the waterbed company: following up to find out why people didn't buy. The auto dealership I was talking about set up a similar system.)

Another example of commando thinking occurred while I was once in Mississauga, Ontario, to assist the Mississauga Board of Trade with telemarketing to increase membership. There were about ten of us (mostly volunteers who had never used the telephone before to market anything) on the phone calling clients. Over a period of a few hours these people became fairly good telemarketers. The biggest thing they got out of it was the realization that if they could do this for the Board, they could go back to their businesses, pick up the telephone, and start calling clients the same way. That was a very exciting thing for them. It was a great experience.

During the recession in 1982, a woman in Burnaby, B.C., took over a service station that was off the beaten track. She had very little money to advertise the place. She just took the telephone book and started calling people and introducing herself. She said she just wanted people to know that she had taken over the station, it was under her management, and it was going to provide good, old-fashioned service. She listed a few of the services she was offering her customers and said that she just wanted to call and invite them in because she'd love to do business with them. She had to stop at page forty of the white pages because she was just too busy to make any more phone calls.

telephone power

The fact is that the telephone is underused. Commando thinking means getting on the phone not just to get new clients, but to talk to your present clients as well. How many of us actually get a call from businesses we deal with to find out how happy we are? It's simple. If you haven't heard from a client in a while, often all they need is a phone call to remind them that they haven't been to see you, and in they come. Anyone can make a phone call like that, but most of us don't. How often has your hair stylist, for example, called you up to ask why you haven't been there lately?

Making a Commitment

I had approval from the Canada Employment Office in Saint John, New Brunswick, to do one of two programs there, but one of the conditions for working in Saint John was to commit to starting a program that included the three smaller markets of St. George, St. Stephen, and St. Andrews. (The government assisted the businesses financially to participate in our entrepreneurial programs.)

I had to sign at least forty businesses to make the program feasible. I had a vice-president in Vancouver and another in Halifax, both of whom said, "Forget it. The market's too small. It won't work." Well, they would have been correct if they had been the ones going in, because if you believe it's not going to work, it won't.

keep your commit-ments

I had made a commitment. It was mid-December, and I had three-and-a-half days, so I went to talk to people in person. Plenty of people told me not to even bother at that time—that you can't sell programs that close to Christmas because people don't want to talk to you. But that was the only time I was free.

I arrived on a Monday afternoon and checked into a motel. I didn't even have an office or a local phone number. I said to myself, "I'm in this market, I've only got three-and-a-half days, nobody knows me here. This is a rural community, and although I am originally from Nova Scotia, which is in Atlantic Canada, as far as these people are concerned I am a big city corporate person coming to town. How do I break into this market, fast?" It obviously wasn't going to just happen. I had to make it happen.

My first realization was that I couldn't do it by myself, coming in with my suit and my attaché case. So I went down and met with the folks at the Canada Employment Office. They were very cooperative. I asked them to introduce me to someone in the community who was well respected, someone who was retired and had some time. They suggested a fellow named Clyde who had just retired from the Central Trust Office, which is both a real estate and a banking organization. The Canada Employment manager called Clyde and set up a meeting. It turned out that Clyde had seen me speak at a real estate conference a couple of years previously, so we did have some kind of relationship and we got along fine.

sometimes it is who you are with

I hired Clyde. I paid him by the day and asked him simply to walk around town with me, to be seen with me. We stopped in together at various businesses, and Clyde would say, "Hello, Charlie." Charlie would say, "Hello, Clyde. I hear you retired. What are you up to these days?" And Clyde would say, "I am working for a few days for Bill Gibson here, who is in from Vancouver. He is with a company called Newport Marketing, and he's setting up a program that's going to be very, very good for this community—and probably would be very good for your business. Charlie, have you got a couple of minutes to give to Bill?" Then Charlie would say, "For you, Clyde, anything."

This gave me the opportunity to sit down and explain the entrepreneurial program. In three-and-a-half days we had eighteen clients signed up and had hired a business advisor for the area who had a lot more leads. In less than three weeks Clyde had signed the forty businesses we needed.

Now that is commando thinking. It's making a commitment, moving quickly into a market, departing from the standard, and bringing in the innovative.

Remaining Innovative

Commando thinking and commando marketing are difficult for competitors to detect or copy—especially if you continue to introduce new strategies.

Twelve years ago I accepted the challenge of managing a faltering radio station on the East Coast of Canada. How tough were things at that station? I describe it (tongue in cheek) as a number five station in a two-station market! The number one station was owned by the well-established Nathansen family, who seemed to have an unlimited amount of capital. They had beautiful facilities, company vehicles, double the number of news and sports staff, both AM and FM frequencies, much stronger radio signals, and in most cases, more experienced on-air, support and sales staff.

Within thirty days I recruited a group of commandos. Some had previously worked for the competitors; others had experience in bigger markets and were seasoned survivors from other fields. What did they have in common? They enjoyed fighting the Goliaths in life, and they were flexible and innovative.

Being a nonunionized station (the competitor was unionized and had restrictions), we immediately shortened the on-air shifts for each announcer. We had them use that same time for getting involved with the community. We were everywhere. We were selling apples with the Boy Scouts and Girl Guides, volunteering deejaying at schools and nonprofit association functions, racing horses at the track, participating in celebrity stock car races, leading parades, performing at the circus, teaching people how to dance, and coordinating outrageous client and station promotions.

Within three months the competition had to add sports and news staff to stay ahead of us. We recruited dozens of volunteer students, miners, retailers, coaches, and parents to be our eyes and ears of the marketplace in return for the coverage and community assistance we gave. It was not uncommon to arrive at the radio station on a Sunday and find 50 percent of our staff working—for no pay.

In six months we increased our local listening audience by 35 percent, came within 13,000 listeners of the number one radio station, and increased our revenue by 250 percent. Commando thinking was the tool that we used.

Becoming a Commando Thinker

I'm sure that the question in your mind at this point is: "How do I become more of a commando thinker to turn my organization into a commando-type organization?" Here are six suggestions:

1. Catch the competitor sleeping. Timing can be everything. Several times our company opened programs, with government assistance for the clients, right under the nose of the local community college. In Canada most of the community colleges have a major political influence on where government training dollars go. The majority of dollars usually flow to them, and many of them don't take kindly to private training companies moving in on government funding.

   In several communities we made our contacts during the summer, when the college staff was on vacation. We also aligned ourselves with the Chamber of Commerce or Boards of Trade to deliver this valuable community training. We then invited community college participation in September. In most cases they refused, but they were not in a position to stop our momentum. We used commando tactics in our timing and in the community partners we selected.

By the way, over the years Newport has had excellent business relations with colleges such as Confederation College in Thunderbay, Fraser Valley College in B.C., and Canador College in Timmins, Ontario. We always welcome amiable business relationships with colleges and universities throughout North America. Our business development programs can be operated through the college system.

2. Look for ways to use volunteer contacts like we did at the radio station. This will expand your marketing power.
3. Hire a few commandos strictly for commando-type jobs. They are usually people who like to fight against the odds or work for a cause. Environmentalists who confront the big timber companies are people with a cause. They use sensationalism and publicity; they are winning more than losing these days.
4. Put the telephone at the top of your list as a commando marketing tool. Think about all the ways you could use the telephone over and above the ways the competition is using it. Put together a commando phone strategy.
5. Look for creative ways to use a mailing list to contact customers and potential customers. Once again, this method is not as visible as other forms of media.
6. Think of what you can do on location or during a call with posters, lists, or giveaways that will give you an advantage in the marketplace.

Commando thinking is marketing, and a big part of marketing, if you want to break it down, is selling. You need to have an organization in which everybody sells and understands the need to sell.

Questions to ask yourself:

- What assets (wall space, reputation, special talents, business contacts) could we be using more effectively?
- What could we do to spend more time with customers to add genuine assistance?
- What high-impact, inexpensive commando moves could we implement in our business?
- What are ten commando moves that I have seen other businesses use? How can we transfer those concepts to our business?

CHAPTER
SEVEN

Everyone Needs to Sell

In Chapter 1, I talked about the outdoor program TREK that my son Shane was part of last year at Prince of Wales High School in Vancouver. The most impressive thing about TREK to me was the responsibility that it put on the students. The government does not pay for all the costs of operating TREK for a year. The students raise a good portion of the expenses through fund raising events and selling various items such as the "Solid Gold Book of Coupons" and Christmas trees at the Arbutus Shopping Center.

During Shane's Christmas in TREK, the students sold over $30,000 worth of trees. About the third day into their sales thrust, I asked him how it was going. He said, "Okay, Dad, but a few of the other students were upset with me." He explained to me that they felt he was too pushy with the customers. Shane was greeting customers immediately and offering to assist them. The rest of the students felt that he should let them walk around for a while before approaching them. Shane disagreed. They won the discussion, and Shane sat back and watched them at work. He said, "Dad, I saw people come in, walk around, and leave. Nobody talked to them. And the other students got very little response from the customers when they did approach them."

So Shane said to heck with it, and he did it his way. I asked him how he was doing. His answer was, "I'm outselling most other students by a huge margin." I assumed it was because he greeted people immediately. His reply was, "Dad, it isn't that simple!" He explained that when customers came on the tree lot, he would skip up to them with a smile on his face and say, "May I help you find a Christmas tree tonight?" Most people would say, "No thanks, I'm just looking." I asked Shane what he did then. He said, "Dad, I just politely let on that I didn't hear them. I then say 'Is it a tall tree, short tree, full tree, or thin tree you are looking for?' " Amazingly enough, according to Shane, they would always answer. He would then say "Follow me" and begin to walk, and they'd follow him to those trees. Just as they got to the trees he'd say, "And how much money do you have to spend on your tree tonight?" They'd give him a figure, and he'd proceed to find them a tree. Just before they bought, he'd say, "Let me show you one other tree before you buy. It is a real beauty—I just love it." Then he'd show them a tree that was $5 to $15 higher in price. Most people spent the extra dollars.

In between customers, you see, he would find those beauties. He also would go around the lot and position them so that they were easy to see and retrieve. He even watched those who wanted to shop by themselves and needed no help. Once they reached in to pull out a tree he'd say, "Let me help you with that so you won't scratch your hands or get your clothes dirty." People were delighted to have him help.

everyone needs to sell

Shane blew my mind, but most of all he gave me a very secure feeling as a parent. Shane Gibson, in my opinion, does not have to worry about his economic future. He may become an architect, a plumber, an environmentalist, a mechanic, or maybe even a retailer. He will succeed in any field he chooses because he is a sales and marketing person. I believe that we need to go beyond just customer service. In today's economy everyone needs to sell.

The Basics of Selling

There is a story in Canada that goes something like this. A number of years ago, on one of the Canadian Forces bases, the cafeteria was having trouble selling some of the food items. So a consultant was hired to come in and help. The consultant suggested that to increase food sales the cafeteria should have somebody standing there offering the food to people. The managers decided to do some research and try it three different ways.

give me options

One of the food items that wasn't exactly selling like crazy was prunes. The prunes weren't (if you'll forgive the pun) moving. So on the first day, an employee stood by the prunes, looked at everybody, and said, "Would you like a bowl of prunes today?" Surprisingly, 60 percent of the people said, "Yes, please." The other 40 percent said, "No, thanks." The next day he said to people, "You wouldn't like a bowl of prunes today, would you?" That day 80 percent of the people said, "No, thank you." Only 20 percent said, "Yes, please." On the third day he asked, "Would you like one or two bowls of prunes today?" When asked that way, 80 percent of the people said, "I'll have one bowl of prunes. Who on earth would want two bowls?" When given a choice, more people bought. Only 20 percent declined.

That's sales language. If you say, "You don't want any dessert, do you?" chances are the person you are asking is going to say, "No, I don't." But if you say, "Would you like apple or lemon pie today?" chances are that you are going to sell one or the other. For companies to succeed in the 1990s, every single person who works with the company has to be sales-oriented. We need everybody selling. We need secretaries selling. We need truck drivers selling. We need subcontractors selling.

sell during delivery

Reg Wightman, a businessman in Bellingham, Washington, owns a building supply dealership called Windsor Plywood. One day he accompanied the truck driver on a delivery. He walked around the site and talked to various people working on the job. When he left the site, he had a bigger order than when he arrived. It made him realize that the person doing the delivery is also really a salesperson. So Reg rearranged his operations. He delegated a lot of his responsibilities as manager to other employees and arranged his time to be on the delivery truck a lot more. His sales increased markedly.

call back after a delivery

When Terry Straker had his waterbed company in Calgary (see Chapter 2), the delivery people carried hoses, drains, and sheets in the truck that they could sell on the spot. Installers were also trained to look around the house and report any needs they noted in terms of furniture. A few days later, one of the salespeople might give a call saying, "When the fellow was in there he noticed you seemed to need . . . ." They got a lot of add-on sales that way. That's a sales organization.

Think about it. If a receptionist answers your telephone, does he or she know about the products and services you offer? A receptionist with the right personality can handle a lot of requests and can make the difference between a client calling back and hanging up. We need to set our organizations up as sales organizations.

Business Cards

business cards for everyone

The first and most important point in business is that everybody sells. So, right from the start, everybody in the business—secretaries, truck drivers, service representatives, and so on—should have personalized business cards with their names typeset on them. They meet people outside the business, so teach them how to use business cards effectively.

cards sell cars

The staff of an automobile dealership in Calgary went to a local restaurant on a regular basis, and they decided to start giving their cards away while they were there. Whenever they left a tip, they left a card with it. It was a fairly big restaurant. In two months they sold five cars to staff members and management, just through that one simple act.

business cards motivate

You might think that giving all your employees business cards is costly. Some people say that you should wait a few months before you give somebody business cards just to make sure that they are going to stay with you. Otherwise, it's a waste of money. But compare the outlook of somebody who's brand new on the job with that of somebody who has been with you for six years. Who is going to give away more cards? The person who just started, of course, because he or she is going to be more excited, even thrilled, to have a new job. New employees are motivated. They run around telling everybody about their new jobs. Three or four weeks later they get to know you, and the excitement wears off. So take advantage of those first weeks—give them business cards early. Remember, a business card is a form of recognition. Not only is it effective in getting customers but it also makes the people who work in your business feel good about themselves. If you can't afford a raise, try giving business cards. It works!

react quickly

And speaking about business cards and selling, I should tell you about the printer who came to one of my seminars. I was making the point about the importance of cards and his hand shot up. "Anybody here who needs business cards gets the first hundred free," he said. Just like that. He did a lot of networking in the group; it was costly, but it was advertising. Beautiful.

one per day

There was a photographer in Abbotsford, British Columbia—Andrew Simpson, principal of Clearbrook Photographic—who made it a goal to give out five business cards per day, every day. His recognition and reputation have spread greatly as a result.

If your business is more product-oriented than service-oriented, you can make your products into business cards. A gift shop in British Columbia, for example, attaches a little sticker to every item. It includes the phone number and this message: "I came from Holly Tree Place in Harrison Hot Springs, B.C." with the phone number. The shop gets calls from all over North America to order gifts because of those little stickers. So, business cards are for everybody—maybe even every*thing*—because everybody sells.

The design of business cards is important, too. Remember, it is the impression a potential customer takes home.

Generating Leads

you need leads

Unfortunately, selling isn't something that comes naturally to everybody. "Who do I talk to?" and "Where do I start?" are common questions novice salespeople often ask. The first step is prospecting. How do salespeople generate leads? Advertising—radio, television, newspapers—is probably the most common way to generate leads. But the imaginative salesperson goes well beyond that.

use directories

Directories are a terrific tool—city directories, Chamber of Commerce memberships, the Yellow Pages, professional associations. Access to the Women's Business Association directory, for example, is great not only for an office supply store, but also for a fine clothing store that caters to women. An advantage to directories is that a membership list or directory leads you both to businesses and to the individuals who run them. They usually list not only the company name, address, and telephone numbers, but also the owner and key contact people.

spend your effort wisely

If you are just flipping through a telephone book, you find company names but you don't know who the people are. Unless you can find out early who the decision maker is, you'll waste a lot of time talking to the wrong people. The phone number is only half the battle. You have to know whom to ask for.

warm call

One way to get such lists is to join the associations. For example, at Newport Marketing, we have often had somebody in the organization who belongs to Meeting Planners International. This is legitimate—we *are* meeting planners—and it also gives us access to all the Meeting Planners International lists for North America. We can then use them for direct mail or phone calls or whatever. If we had a sales representative personally call on each of the meeting planners in the directory and represent me or some of our other speakers, it would generate plenty of leads. The membership in the association also helps to open the door; your sales rep and client are members of the same association, which makes it a "warm call" versus a "cold call."

subscription lists

Subscription lists are another source of leads. If you are running a clothing store, for example, the subscribers to *Style* magazine (or something similar) would be a great place to start.

Obtaining Referrals

present customer base

Your existing customers are another great source of leads. If they are happy with your business, they will probably tell their friends about you. Such referrals are the best way to generate new leads. Leveraged referrals, which are referrals from people whom you know, respect, and trust, are even more powerful than regular referrals.

Brian Small, the manager of the Greater Victoria Chamber of Commerce, who was the vice president of the Chamber of Commerce Executives of Canada, endorsed me as Canada's top business speaker. He sent a letter on his letterhead to the rest of the Chamber of Commerce executives and 40 percent of them contacted me. I ended up with about $80,000 worth of business from an $800 investment, which was absolutely phenomenal. That is what you would call a leveraged referral.

At this point, many of you reading this might be thinking to yourselves, "Yes, but how do you ask for referrals in the first place?" Let me give an example of someone we hired to build referrals in a community where we were marketing one of our owner development programs. After two or three weeks, we knew he was the wrong person. He was spending all of his time talking to bankers and lawyers, getting leads to go out and sell an eight- to ten-month training program in a community of maybe 30,000. I felt he was wasting his time. He should have been out there cold calling—talking to the businesspeople, the store owners.

everyone is a reference

So we hired Ron Beveridge. He was eager to do the job right. I filled him in on the previous situation, and he asked, "Well, how do I get the leads?" We were driving along the main street at the time. I stopped the car and said, "Do you see any businesses here?" He said, "I see dozens and dozens of businesses." I said, "Well, why do you need leads? Get out of the car and start. I am going to give you your first lead—there's Joe's shoe store. Walk in and say Bill Gibson sent you. And he'll say, 'Who's Bill Gibson?' and off you go."

I continued, "Before you do five calls, you will find at least one or two people who are really friendly and who will like you, even though they don't buy from you. You say 'Look, I'm new here in town and I wasn't sure where to start, so I thought I would start right here on this block. Do you know anybody who might like this program who I can go and see?' Each one of those people who's friendly with you will give you two or three names. Some will even pick up the phone and call people for you. That's lead generation. You don't have to go find any lead organizations or anything. When somebody really likes you, you say, 'Can I use your name as one of the people who really endorses this program?' They say yes, and before you know it, you have five or six people endorsing the whole thing. Suddenly you have a lead team going." It's like starting a snowball rolling.

always ask

Many salespeople forget to ask for referrals. We talk about learning to farm the market, not hunt the market. Don't hunt the market for sales; farm the market for referrals to future sales. The best time to ask for referrals is after the sales presentation. Tell the person you are trying to get a referral from about the product or service you are involved in, and say, "So you probably would know some people who might be interested in the product or service." You're not just trying to sell to that person; you're also trying to get some referrals.

Often I phone a business and say, "We always begin in a community by calling the most progressive businesspeople in town. When speaking with other people in town (you may even name a few people), your name keeps coming up. I'm confident that you will be interested in what I am going to talk about."

Even if you don't make a sale, you might make three sales from the information he or she gives you. So you talk to people, you ask them things. It's different from what we used to call "awning calls." Every store had an awning that they rolled out in front of the store. It would say, for example, "Pete's Poolroom," or "Joe Smith, proprietor," at the end of the awning. Salespeople would be told that they had to make X number of calls per day and then had to report the names and stores of the people they had called on. If their quota was fifteen calls, they might do five real ones and then ten awning calls because they could do them while driving down the street. That's what happens when you put quantity of calls over quality. It is not uncommon at the end of a day to hear statements from salespeople such as, "I didn't make a sale, but I got fifteen calls in today." Or even, "I made twenty-two calls today. I could have made more but one client bought, and it slowed me down."

Sometimes people are reluctant to share their contacts with you, or are shy about having their names used. That doesn't mean that they are of no help to you. Maybe they will give you a name but don't want their names mentioned. A way to use that referral is to have fun with it. Use "a little bird told me" letter or "the grapevine" or "a little mouse." If it is cute and light, it will work.

go for the phone numbers

One method that has worked very well for me when I have obtained referrals in the past is to ask for not just the name and company I am being referred to but also the phone number. A lot of salespeople say that's kind of stupid. Why would you do that? You can look it up in the telephone book. Are you lazy? However, besides saving time, if you ask for the telephone number you may get a number that's a direct line to the decision maker, as opposed to the general business phone. You could look up the address in the telephone book, but when *they* flip to *their* telephone directory they open a whole book to *you*. Rather than getting one referral you may get four or five, because as they go through the book they are going to pass by the names of other people who might also be interested in your product or service.

personal message on a card

One of the best ways to break the ice when you first step into an office is the personal-message-on-a-business-card method. You go into an office and say, "Rick Gibson-Shaw sent me over to see Mr. Davidson." Then you hand the secretary Gibson-Shaw's card. On the back of the card there is a note from Rick that reads, "Bob, I think that it is important that you see Bill." You ask the secretary to take it to Mr. Davidson and tell him that you are there to see him. It's from Mr. Gibson-Shaw, who is a good friend of his.

There are three steps to the personal-message-on-a-business-card strategy: (1) Ask for the business card at the end of your presentation to the buyer (hopefully you have closed the sale); (2) ask for names of people who the buyer thinks would be interested in your product or service; and (3) request that the buyer write a quick note to the referred client on the back of the card. Then you take that card to the referred business.

Using the Telephone

One of the most common mistakes that people make when they are outbound selling is trying to sell the product or service over the telephone. Most high-ticket or high-value products and services require more explanation and should not be sold over the phone. You can sell cassettes of Christmas songs over the telephone with some backup TV advertising, but you can't sell small business owner development programs worth $3,800 over the phone. Use the phone to sell the appointment. Then use the appointment to sell the product or service.

sell the appointment

Most people have an aversion to using the telephone to sell, but once they do use it they feel it's easier than actually going face to face with the customer and dealing with the presentation the way it should be done. If it only takes half an hour to make the full presentation, all you need to sell on the phone is the thirty minutes—the appointment—not the product or service.

Most likely you will phone somebody and they will want to know exactly what you are calling about. Try not to complicate things for them by giving out too much information on the phone. Stick to the basics. I usually say, "I'd love to explain to you but it will be tough on the phone." They say, "If you can't tell me on the telephone then I'm not interested in hearing about it." So I reply, "Well, I got your name from so and so who said you were a progressive businessperson who loved ways to increase business. Obviously you don't have a lot of time right now. When would be a better time to call you? It is a concept that will make you money."

be there in five

Give the client an option on times, otherwise you could go on forever trying to pin down a time. "Is this afternoon or tomorrow okay?" If you get a third objection as to when you could get together, you can say, "Mrs. Smith, if it would help you I could be there in minutes. I'll make the presentation short." This is where cellular phones are so powerful—you can be sitting out in front of the store and say, "If I could be there in five minutes could you see me? I'll bring some coffee with me." You have her on the phone so you know she's there. But it is important that you do not use this tactic until you have already tried to arrange a meeting at least a couple of times. I have found that no matter what market I go to or how many sales people tell me that everything's different in their community, two things are always the same: (1) People who come into a retail store are always, no matter what you say to them, "just looking"; and (2) businesspeople are *always* busy. People say that they are just looking or that they are busy because they are so used to being handled poorly by salespeople that they would rather do things and find things for themselves, even if it means not buying anything.

people are always just looking or too busy

Busy businesspeople may not give me an appointment; however, when I drop in for a surprise visit, they usually have their feet up on the desk and don't even remember talking to me. You have to expect that they are always going to be busy. They will be too busy to see you today, they will be too busy to see you tomorrow, and they will probably be too busy to see you the next day. But your success lies in how you word things and the value you offer. Ask them whether they are too busy to hear some new ideas or a concept that made money for a related business in another market. (Only say this if it is the truth; otherwise, it is a con.)

Ironically, the busiest people are going to be your best customers—if you can get in to make your presentation. These people are so busy that most other salespeople cannot get in to see them. But if you can get in to present your product or service, you'll have the field to yourself. The competition will have a tough time breaking through the guard system.

In my seminar, when I ask what people would do if their company stopped all the usual methods of generating leads as a corporation, putting the onus completely on the employees, a few people say they would place ads in the newspaper, but nine people out of ten say, "I'd get on the phone." People know what a powerful tool the phone is. Yet, if a manager were to say to the sales team or to the delivery people or to the clerks sitting around in a store on a slow day, "Pick up the phone and let's start going through the telephone book to generate some business," what would the response be? "That's not my job. That's not what I do." Well, maybe that is what they *should* do!

telephone lowers advertising costs

Bridgeport Carpets, which does well over $30 million worth of business a year in western Canada, recently cut its advertising dollars from about $1.5 million a year to around $250,000 while increasing its sales. Instead of advertising, the firm focused on phone work, on customer service, and on follow-through marketing. Whenever a manager phones from one of the stores and says, "We need to do some advertising," the first question the head office asks is, "Well, what are you doing on the phone today?"

Networking

The scope of networking is incredible. To give you an idea, consider the study that was done in the 1970s in which people in the United States were asked to try to get envelopes delivered to particular people in Africa. They had to pass the envelope on to people they knew personally, who could pass it on to people they knew, and so on until it got to someone who actually knew the person in Africa and could deliver it there. The study tracked how many times each envelope changed hands before it got from a randomly chosen American to a randomly chosen African through people who knew each other. On the average the envelope changed hands five times. Apparently, a similar study was done with envelopes going from the West Coast of the United States to the East Coast. They got there faster than they did through the post office. That's the power of networking.

networking

Imagine that your company stopped all advertising, took the sign off the front of the store, took its name out of the Yellow Pages, removed all the "normal" customer traffic. What could you do to generate new business? What if you were in a really tight financial spot and didn't have the money and leverage to join associations or run advertising or buy a directory or even rent one? You would need to start networking. You would sit down with the staff and see what kind of options everybody had for finding leads and referrals.

Other Methods

There are lots of other ways to generate leads, including trade shows and the daily paper. Watch for ads from other businesses to see who's new in town. New businesses usually use the newspaper because the Yellow Pages only come out once a year.

new business, new leads

Another method I used when I sold advertising for a radio station was to meet each month with several businesspeople who were in the market of selling business machines, office supplies, and so on. They always knew what businesses were about to open. Large contractors are also good contacts for this information. Attorneys who register corporate names are another good source. You can get a list of the new companies that have been incorporated each month.

An excellent place to get leads is from your competitors. I used to sit down with my competitors—there was usually someone in each company who I really liked—and we would trade advice. When I sold advertising with CJCH/C100 FM (CHUM Group of Companies), I used to meet with Herb Jordan from CFDR and with George MacLeod of CHNS (Halifax). The biggest competitor for new accounts is often your colleague, the person sitting next to you, because once a coworker gets an account, you are not allowed to call on it. But if the competitor gets the account, you can go call on it! So I often spent time *with the competitors*, exchanging information. A word of caution, however: You should not exchange information that could adversely affect your sales counterparts, clients, or company.

start where it makes sense

Public information can also be used to generate leads. It all depends on the business you are in. If you are in the life insurance business, for example, go through the new birth notices. If you are in the diaper cleaning delivery service, start at the hospital or ask a salesperson at a maternity clothing store. That's being a step ahead! Consider your customer's competitors as well. For example, you can call similar companies and say, "You know, we are doing this for ABC Company, and we can do the same for you very easily." By the same token, remember that if you are buying from suppliers and you really don't want them selling to your competitors, you should put that in your contract.

seminar leads

Another way to find leads is to hold your own seminars. Financial planners do it all the time, and there's no reason that it can't happen in a building supply business or in a ladies' wear shop.

If I were to run a building supply store, for example, I would build a permanent stage in one corner of the store and have weekly formal demonstrations of drywalling and plumbing and electrical wiring. I would have it there every weekend so that people would know when and where. They would flock to the business.

My theory is that if you educate your customers, you'll never have to knock your competition because they'll end up knocking themselves.

I was giving a talk once with Neil Godin in northern B.C. about the importance of holding seminars for clients to educate them. A woman who owned a real estate firm raised her hand and said, "We have a problem because a lot of people are starting to sell their own homes and we lose business." I said, "Well, why don't you help them? Why don't you put on a seminar on how to sell your own home without a realtor?" She replied, "You mean, a real estate company showing people how to sell a house without a realtor?" I said, "Yes, once you give someone time plus sincere assistance, you've got a relationship of one degree or another that equals a commitment from both parties."

She tried it. The firm brought in a local contractor to tell people how to fix up their homes, somebody else to talk about landscaping, a banker to talk about financing, and an appraiser to tell people how to value their homes. She herself spoke about showing homes. Out of about thirty home owners that showed up for the seminar, ten ended up listing their homes with her company. When they saw what it really took to sell a home, they said, "I don't want to have to do all this. You people seem very nice, how about you listing my home?"

If you are the best trained and the sharpest in your area of business, you are going to succeed. It's all about sticking your neck out a little bit; you have to say, "How do we really help the customer through the seminars that we are doing?" If you are truly there to assist, you'll get the return.

Strategies of an Effective Salesperson

Most major banks and telephone companies go through a lot of training in service quality. However, they are now realizing that it isn't good enough to simply give service. They have to know how to sell.

the tougher it is, the less the competition

I was doing a session with B.C. Tel for its customer service reps, who were trying to change from a service philosophy to a more sales-oriented philosophy. A lot of the people in that audience said, "I wasn't hired to be a salesperson. I was hired to do this. I don't like selling." I told them, "How would you like to have security for the rest of your life? Look at the people who are losing their jobs today. Ask a salesperson who really knows how to sell if she or he is afraid of being laid off. He or she will say 'No. I will just get another job.' If B.C. Tel closed down tomorrow, what would you do? You may be a qualified engineer, but if you don't know how to sell your services, how are you going to survive? What if you want to leave the company you work for and open a small business? People who open small businesses and know how to sell have a phenomenal chance of success."

The daily newspaper always lists dozens and dozens of sales jobs available in its classified sections. In bad times there are even more, which is very interesting. Professional salespeople create their own job security. Most companies will train people in product knowledge, but they have difficulty training professional salespeople because selling is an art. To be an effective salesperson, you must practice your technique and find your own style. It takes time and money to train people, and a lot of business can be lost during that training period.

Effective salespeople choose what company they work for, what town they live in, and basically what their income will be relative to how hard they are willing to work. Selling is the highest-paid hard job and the lowest-paid easy job in the world.

practice works

Betty Davidson, for example, had never sold anything. She had always worked looking after her husband, Bob—and that was a lot of work. Betty had always told Bob that some day she would like to have an organ. She had learned to play the piano years ago. When Bob got a bonus of $1,000 for sales and marketing excellence, he went down to the Yamaha store and asked them what kind of organ he could buy for $1,000. They had one on sale for $999.95. It was perfect. Amazingly, Betty completely outgrew that organ in two months. It was totally inadequate. So they went back and bought a $3,000 organ. Soon after that the fellow who owned the store phoned Betty and asked her if she had ever considered demonstrating and selling organs. She told them that she had never done anything like that in her life—she had no previous experience. After the conversation, he hired her.

The store sent her away on a two-day training course with Yamaha in Winnipeg, and she came home with a thick manual. When Bob asked her how it was, she said that it was the biggest waste of time she had ever been involved in. It was all nonsense, and it would never work.

put it in your own words

The next night Betty and Bob sat down together and went through the manual and role-played. As time went by, Betty started to put the material in her own words. All of a sudden the mystery disappeared and the common sense appeared. She went to work and began using the processes in the manual in her own words. Until she took the academic aspect out of it and made it practical, it wouldn't work.

In many instances, this is true for phone soliciting as well. People are set up with a script that doesn't even sound like them. No matter how many times they say it, it doesn't sound like them, and the person on the other end of the phone feels as if she's talking to a machine.

Unfortunately, people think that they have to go into a different mode in order to represent something. In other words, they believe they have to learn to be something they are not. This is not true. In fact, being yourself and having fun are very important.

make it fun

Bob Davidson has to make selling fun because he doesn't like doing it. He continually looks for different ways to talk to people. For example, he will go into a store and when somebody comes up and asks, "Can I help you?" he says, "If a salesperson came in here and it was absolutely mandatory that he be thrown out of the store, who's the final authority for throwing him out?" "Well, that would be the owner," the employee replies. "Well, would you go there and tell him that there is a salesman in the store who needs to be thrown out?" That staff member will go to the owner with a grin and chuckle. Sure enough, the owner will come out of the office to see who needs to be thrown out.

Another strategy Bob uses is to call someone and say, "My name's Bob Davidson, and I'm with Newport Marketing. I've got something that I know is going to be of interest to you, but I've got a terrible problem. I don't know how to get to see you. So I'd appreciate it if you told me how a guy that's calling you can get to see you." The person on the other end of the phone will say, "Well, I guess he asks if he can come over." "Hey, can I come over?" Usually they let him. Bob changes his strategy every time, and that's what makes it fun. But notice that he is doing the right thing: He is selling the appointment, not the product. And he is being himself.

what is a call worth?

Those who fear the rejection that is part of the sales process should consider the following illustration: Let's say that the average commission of a salesperson on a car lot is $250. If every sale is worth $250 and it takes five presentations to make a sale, then every presentation is worth $50. Let's also say that it takes ten phone calls, business cards, or referrals to get people to come to the lot. Each call, card, or referral is worth $5. What if your company wrote you a check for $5 every time you picked up the phone to make a call to see if somebody wanted to buy a car, or every time that you were out at the Kiwanis Club or the Chamber of Commerce meeting and you handed a card to somebody who might buy a car? How many cards would you hand out? How many calls would you make? A lot of them, right? Now if that doesn't overcome the fear of rejection, I don't know what does. The problem with most people is that they get concerned about how much they make on a sale. They don't think about how much they make every time they simply mention what they do.

People who aren't on commission have to learn that their salaries are basically the same sort of thing. If we are just order takers, then our salaries reflect the fact that we are just order takers. If we are salespeople and we are really out there taking the initiative to sell, it won't be long until our salaries and promotions reflect the fact that we are salespeople.

Qualifying Buyers

ready, willing, and able

Usually, people who complain about not being able to close deals don't know how to qualify their buyers. If you are not qualifying your buyer early in the presentation, then there is no way that you're going to close it. To qualify—that is, to change somebody from a suspect into a real prospect—

you have to know three things about them: You need to know the need, the desire, and the ability to pay. Another way to think of it is how ready, willing, and able your buyers are. You have to qualify those things early in the presentation or there is no sense in going on. The customer must be ready and willing to take ownership, and he or she must be able to pay.

If any of these three components is missing, it is our job in selling to determine whether it's missing because we are not doing our job or whether it's missing because customers don't have the need, desire, or ability to pay. If they don't have one of those three things, there is no sense in closing because it will come back to haunt you. It is possible, through some of these techniques, to sell things to people that they don't want, don't need, and can't afford. You can sell a Cadillac to someone who can't afford a bicycle, but you won't get the money. You will have a collection problem. Or, even if they can afford it, they might then go home and decide that they don't have a need for it. So cut the problems—qualify properly.

Closing the Sale

When you sell things, you sell the benefits combined with the features, the products, and the services. If you are selling a coffee cup, the fact that it has a handle will not sell a whole lot of cups. But if you say it has a handle that allows you to put several fingers in so you don't drop it, that's important. Customers buy the benefit, not the feature, and that's the important thing when you are selling any product or service.

answer with a question

When you're making presentations, sell features and benefits, but also handle the objections that everybody will have. Always answer an objection with a question. Somebody once asked Sammy Davis, Jr., "Why do you Jewish people always answer a question with a question?" He said, "What makes you think I am Jewish?"

Professional salespeople must get in the habit of answering questions with questions. That's what I call 70/30 selling. Question, absorb, and listen 70 percent of the time, and explain your product and service 30 percent of the time—at the maximum. A 90/10 ratio might be an even better target.

Telling does not equal selling. Salespeople are often trained to memorize their pitch or their presentation so that they end up telling rather than selling. So question, question, question, especially when somebody makes an objection. For example, if they say that it costs too much, you can respond by saying, "I am sure you have a reason for feeling that way. Do you mind if I ask what it is?" or "How much is too much?" or "How far apart are we?" Don't ask, "How much do you feel you can afford?" That's an open-ended question, and it won't get you the answers you want. The best thing to ask is, "How high is too high?" When someone says $200, then you don't sell the $400 item, you sell the $200 difference. For example, you say, "Well, let me show you what the $200 represents. This is what you are getting for the extra $200."

Here's another example. Let's say that a business speaker thinks that your rates as a professional editor and writer are a bit high, say by $10 an hour. He or she probably has not considered everything. For the extra $10 this is what the speaker is getting: As an editor you have direct contact with publishers; you know what they are looking for. You have also worked for several other business speakers. That's what the speaker is getting for the extra $10 an hour. After you explain it, the speaker will probably agree that you're worth it.

When somebody is considering the Newport Program and says that it costs too much, I respond, "At Newport we made a conscious decision when we started this program. We decided that we would justify the price once rather than make excuses for poor quality forever."

Beyond Technique

It is important to remember that selling isn't just technique. Most of us succeed in spite of our great skills. We often believe that we have succeeded because of our skills. I've often watched people come out of a meeting and say, "Did you see how skillful I was?" Clients often take the deal while still seeing the close coming. They saw how the product or service was used and decided to buy simply because they liked the salesperson or the product. We all have a tendency to believe that we succeed because of our technique, but the truth is that we succeed most often because a relationship was developed through trust, respect, or entertainment. We don't realize that the person saw through our intellectual moves and decided that he or she liked the person within.

For example, Beverley, my wife, and I were shopping for furniture. We wanted to buy a sofa and a love seat. We went all around town and shopped and shopped and shopped until we finally hit on a furniture store where the sales clerk was incredibly helpful. He was good at his job. He was helpful, and he educated us on buying furniture. Even when we were comparing the furniture, he didn't take us to another piece that was higher priced, he took us to one of equal price and showed us the difference in the way the two pieces were made. Then he took a run at a close. When he saw that we didn't move, he said, "Well, that's sort of a trial close." He was lighthearted about his technique. We ended up buying the furniture from him, not because of his skill, but because of his personality. We could see his sincerity among the skills he was using. People are more persuaded by the depth of your sincerity than the height of your logic and skills.

There is a saying in the sales business that "he who answers first loses." You have to be careful with such statements because they are only general rules. But general rules such as these have made robots of many salespeople who follow them, and that's why most of these people have never reached the level of sales they've desired. They haven't learned that the real thing that sells is the heart and sincerity.

In fact, the first person who speaks doesn't necessarily lose. You may be dealing with a quiet person who needs prodding, and you may have to speak first to guide the discussion and close the deal. The reason to be silent is so that you don't pressure the customer—it is to show courtesy and to allow the person time to think and make a decision. That's why you say to a couple who are trying to make a decision, "Look, I am going to leave you here for a few minutes because I can see that you have something you want to talk about. I am going to have a coffee, and I'll come back in five minutes." That's the silent close, and it's one of courtesy because you care about your customer.

Remember I said that you can sell things to people that they don't want, don't need, and can't afford—and they usually bring them back? The technical skills that you use to sell can be manipulative. As soon as they become manipulative, all those skills are like a gun in the hand of a child. They are dangerous. There are times when you may want to manipulate somebody toward something that you know is really good for them, and once they are into it you say, "I did manipulate you into this, but I could see that you really needed it." They usually turn around and say, "Thank you for dragging me in here because this is the best thing that has ever happened to me." However, that part of selling is something that you have to be careful of. It is like selling a child on a different choice of friends.

To be successful, people in business must become comfortable with the idea of thinking of themselves as people who are in the world of selling. If you are alive, you are in sales. If you go home on a Friday night and you want to go out and your spouse does not want to go with you, you are in sales. If you arrive home three hours late for dinner, you are in sales. If you want to go to the bank to borrow some money, you are in sales. If the tax person arrives at your door, you are in sales. If you want a raise in pay, you are in sales. We're all in sales, and we have to learn to feel more comfortable with it and use a lot of sales skills, sales philosophies, and sales methods. It's a way of living.

Businesses today really need to be sales-oriented. This book is not big enough to explore every facet of selling, but it is big enough to make you aware that you have to go out now and enroll in training programs, subscribe to sales newsletters, read magazine articles and books on sales, listen to tapes, and above all, make sure that everyone in your business understands the power of selling. If everybody sells, you can boost your business in any economy.

Questions to ask yourself:

- How many of my employees have business cards?
- How could we change our sales language to sell more?
- Who could give me referrals?
- Do I still fear rejection in sales? If so, how can I get over it?
- Am I comfortable with selling? If not, how can I get more comfortable?
- What strategies and training can I implement in my business so that everyone becomes a salesperson?

CHAPTER
EIGHT

United We Stand

When you see geese flying south for the winter, you see them flying in a V formation. Why do they do this? Scientists have found that when each bird flaps its wings it creates an uplift for the bird immediately following it. The whole flock gains a 71 percent greater flying range than if each bird flew alone.

change leaders

You will notice that when a goose falls out of the V it doesn't stay out long. It can really feel the drag, so it gets back into formation, helping to lift the others and move them along. Something else you'll notice is that the leader, the bird at the head of the V, is not the leader for the entire trip south. The geese change leaders. When one leader gets tired it backs off and moves to a different position, and another goose flies up to take the lead.

sticking together

If a goose gets shot or gets sick and it leaves the V, two geese leave with it, follow it down, and look after it on the ground until it either dies or gets well. If the goose dies, they try to catch up with the flock. They don't just leave birds who are in trouble to fend for themselves. They try to help.

In businesses today the traditional hierarchical way of running businesses is not working. We need to make sure that we have lots of leaders in our organizations and that we get our people involved. That way, when the leader does get tired somebody else can step in and head that formation. There is an uplift that carries along everybody who flies in a V. This chapter is about how strong we are when we are united. United we stand.

Dunsmuir Shell

I would like to tell you a mind-blowing story about how powerful we can be in an organization if we are united. A few years ago I was doing a session in Victoria, B.C., and a fellow put up his hand and said, "Bill, you are talking about a super attitude and a real team spirit, combined with great customer service. How would you like to see the best team effort and the most impressive customer service in the world?" I said I would love to. He said, "It's just down the street a ways. Go down and check out the service in this little gas station."

About three days later my wife Beverley and I drove to the service station. I pulled up to the pumps, and the first thing I saw was a young man and a young woman coming across that lot on the run toward my car. The young man got there first. He scared me to death! I had never seen anybody come at my car like that. He said, "Fill her up?" Still recovering from the shock, I said, "Go ahead." He put the nozzle into the gas tank and walked back over to the window. He said, "Look, if it wouldn't be too much trouble for the two of you, I would like to ask you to get out of your car."

surprise me

I was a little nervous about that because the last person who asked me to get out of my car was a highway patrolman. But he said, "No, don't worry about it. I'll just take this big vacuum cleaner here and while you are out of your car, we'll clean it out for you at no charge while you're getting your gasoline."

beyond expectations

Well, if you saw our car you'd understand how quickly we jumped out of it. In seconds they were in there: They cleaned the car out, they washed the windows, they went under the hood, they cleaned the ashtrays, they did everything that most service stations don't do. Believe me, I was knocked out.

the little extra

When I paid him, he gave me a receipt, looked at me, and said, "By the way, this is Friday. Friday's a special day around here. On Fridays, we give the first 250 customers a flower." And he handed my wife a carnation. Beverley looked at me and said, "See, that's how it's done!" I could have belted the guy for that—how to ruin a man's relationship with his wife!

word of mouth

We drove away. An hour after we arrived home, Beverley had told no less than a dozen people about where we got the flower and the kind of service at that service station.

we didn't forget

About three days later my car wouldn't start. I picked up the telephone to call my regular service station, but Beverley intervened. She said, "Bill, call the service station that gave me the flower. If they give that kind of service for a tank of gas, what do they do if there's something really wrong with your car?"

help me

Well, I called the service station. Within a couple of minutes the mechanic determined that it was probably my battery. He offered to come out and help me, but I said I had jumper cables and would use them to start the car. I took the car down to the gas station. One of their employees drove me home and said he'd call in 30 minutes. In exactly 30 minutes the phone rang. The mechanic said that the battery was completely gone. Wiped out. He said, "It looks fairly new. I think you bought the battery at one of our chain's stations. Check to see if you have a warranty." I checked, and they were right. I had bought it at their chain, and I had a warranty on it. The new battery cost me $18.

the little things

When my car was returned, it had been washed and vacuumed. They even tightened up the rearview mirror, which had been dangling for three years. I was impressed.

Six weeks later I was on the prairies in Weyburn, Saskatchewan—about 1600 miles east of Victoria. I was talking to eighty general managers of gas stations. I told them about the service station and asked them, "How many of you people have ever had service like that in a gas station?"

Two hands went up. I asked the first guy where it was. He said Victoria, B.C. I asked how long ago. He said about a year and a half ago, and I said, "Well, do you remember the name of the service station?" At this point I hadn't mentioned the name. He said, "Dunsmuir Super Service Shell." I asked how on earth he remembered the name of that service station after a year and a half. He said, "Bill, how on earth could I ever forget? We pulled up to those pumps in a forty-eight seat bus loaded with ball players, and their employees insisted on coming on that bus and vacuuming it from one end to the other."

I asked the second guy who had put up his hand about his experience. He said that he and his wife had been on vacation out in Victoria a year ago. It was definitely Dunsmuir Shell, he said, because they got a flower that day. The only difference was that they got a rose instead of a carnation.

blow their minds

When I went back to Victoria I wanted to meet Bob Dunsmuir. I had never met him, even though I had been in his service station. I wanted to tell him the story about the bus. When I met with Bob, I said, "Bob, I have to tell the story that I heard on the prairies about this bus that came in here and the service you gave them." He said, "I remember that bus. As a matter of fact, I can see those Saskatchewan license plates on that bus pulling in here right now. The funny thing was, the day that that bus pulled in, a couple of the guys from the pumps and a couple of mechanics were sitting here not doing too much. When that bus pulled in, we all looked at each other, and at the same time we said, 'Let's blow their minds.' And we all hit the bus at the same time, five of us. We vacuumed the bus out, we washed the windows, we went under the hood, we checked the tires, we did everything to that bus and blew their minds."

be alert when it is slow

In a lot of businesses it's tough to get good service, even on slow days. You walk into the business, and a couple of people working there are just standing around. One will look at the other and say, "You take him." The other one will say, "No, you take him. I took the last one three days ago." When business is really slow, people don't feel like moving. But here was a company that was having a slow day and took the time to make sure that they really doubled up—quadrupled up—to handle the customer.

show me you care

When it comes to managing our employees and dealing with our customers, we often forget the little things. We often think it is the big things that count, but a little thing like a flower is remembered by a customer. When was the last time you acknowledged somebody who works in your own department with a flower or a small gift? When was the last time you did that for one of your customers?

The Herzberg Theory

About three months after my experience in Weyburn, I was asked to speak to a group of executives and owners of companies at a conference in Victoria, B.C. The attendees were from Oregon, Washington, Idaho, British Columbia, and Alberta. They had asked me to speak on the Herzberg theory of management.

motivating people

According to Herzberg, five things motivate people: (1) recognition, (2) responsibility, (3) advancement, (4) achievement, and (5) the work itself—doing something you love. With those five things in mind, I started to look for an example I could use to illustrate the Herzberg theory (one of the best ways to get a point across is through a story).

I thought of Dunsmuir Super Service Shell, and it occurred to me that Bob Dunsmuir must have some really neat ways of managing people. With the speed that people run around his service station, he must use some unusual methods to motivate them. I figured that he probably used something like the Herzberg theory of management. So I phoned Dunsmuir. I told him, "Bob, I'd like to come down and spend some time with you. I'd like to discuss the Herzberg theory of management."

I went down to see Bob and we sat in the front of his little service station. We started to chat, and I explained to him why I was there—that I wanted to talk about the way he handled his employees. I said to him, "Bob, tell me something: How do you get people to run to the pumps?"

know your team goal

He said, "Well, back a number of years ago we tried to decide what our number one function in this business was. We had a meeting, and at that meeting we determined that our number one function wasn't to pump gasoline or fix automobiles. We determined that the number one function was to make every single customer feel totally wanted."

That is a very basic statement. You can go into Dusmuir Shell and ask any employee, "What's the goal here?" and they'll say, "To make customers feel wanted." It's not ten paragraphs of a mission statement. They know why they are there.

staff input

Next I asked, "Once you came up with making the customers feel wanted, did anything expand from there?" Bob said, "Yeah, one of the first things that one of the young fellows came up with was that if everybody here were to run to the pumps or walk real fast when a customer arrived, the customers would feel wanted immediately. It was the staff that made it part of the job description. They sat there and agreed as a group that all the people who worked there now and anybody that would ever start there would have to agree to run to the pumps or walk fast—or they don't work there. And somebody said, 'Well, what if it's icy outside?' 'Well,' I said, 'Put your skates on. If you walk to the pumps at Dunsmuir Shell, you keep on walking.'"

When the employees came up with this idea, what they were really doing was setting standards. They were working together and being united on the "how to's" of running the business. Our businesses have to have standards. The better the standards, the stronger the team, and the better the customer service.

set standards

My next question to Bob was, "Where do you find good people like this to put such a team together? Do you have any special hiring procedures?" He said, "Yes I do. I only interview people at one time during the day. Seven in the morning. At three o'clock in the afternoon somebody could take four hours getting ready for an interview, and they could come in and fool you. But at 7:00 A.M. if it takes four hours to get ready, they've been up since three and you can tell at a glance! I want people who are ready, willing, and able—motivated. Somebody who really is sharp in the morning because we start early here."

odd time interviews

Bob told me that when he finishes that first interview he often says to the applicant, "I have some things I have to do and I have to get at it. Can you come back again tomorrow morning at seven?" After that next morning he'll say, "Listen, I want somebody else to interview you as well. Can you come back again tomorrow at seven?" He has gone as many as four days in a row to see the commitment and the attitude of the people he puts in there.

be creative when hiring

The attitude of the people is vital when we talk about building a team. If you have a group of people who are all very positive and working well as a team and you add someone who's thinking negative thoughts, the cynical person will draw the energy from the group. That's called psychic pollution, and we've all experienced it.

psychic pollution

Also, when Bob hires someone he does not make the decision by himself. He always gets other employees to be there during an interview because they are the ones who are going to have to work with the person. Then if a mistake is made, Bob is not on the hook by himself. That's the importance of the old "we" instead of the "I" doing everything. If we are united in hiring, we become united in trying to make the right decision.

get more than one opinion

I said, "Well, Bob, how do you keep these people moving?" He said, "Well, one of the things that we do here that's mandatory is that we have a meeting at 5:35 P.M. every Wednesday. And when you start in this business you have to agree to arrive at those meetings. If you don't arrive at a meeting, you don't get to keep your job."

mandatory meetings

The reason for the meetings is that even in small businesses, where we all work with each other and assume that we communicate, we really don't sit down and talk about a lot of the things that have to be hashed out. A meeting gives people a chance to pass the buck or to get some help or support. When you are trying to do everything by yourself, your ego can run wild. When you have people in a room with you, your ego

make meetings interesting

gets balanced and you see things in a different (and usually healthier) way. If your company is not running regular meetings, start now.

open the books

One of the other things that Bob does to keep his people moving is to open up the books on the second Wednesday of every month. He has had the accountant design the books so that he can easily show the employees where the money is being made and where it's not being made. He is educating his people.

have fun

At Bob's service station they have fun, too. The day that I interviewed him, a young native Canadian man who was in charge of the pumps came into work and said to Bob, "I see you are going to lose your service station. I just read in the newspaper there that your service station is on Indian land, and I am going to get it." Bob laughed and so did I. They take the time to keep things light and fun around the service station.

I told that story about the young native man at a speaking engagement a year later at a large shopping center in the same area, and a woman put up her hand and said, "Bill, do you know where that young man is now?" She told me that he is now the manager of the Woolco automotive service department—he won out over several hundred other applicants for the job.

Later, when I interviewed Bob Dunsmuir again, he confirmed this information. He said, "Well, I had heard that he was going for this job. I called him in, and we sat down and had a good talk because I wanted to make sure it wasn't anything I had done that made him want to leave. The young man said he didn't have a problem, but he really saw it as an opportunity, which I could understand."

So Bob picked up the phone, called the manager of Woolco, and told him very clearly that he'd be making a big mistake if he didn't hire this young fellow. He was the man for the job. How do you think the rest of the staff felt when they heard that the owner of the company had helped someone get this great job? That's a supportive environment!

Bob tells employees about the opportunity for advancement. He says, "Your opportunity for advancement is that the next customer that comes in here could be your next boss. So serve them well—then maybe you can get out of here." Bob described a few more people to me. A couple of them had jobs as managers of Shell self-serve stations and a couple more had ended up with a general insurance company in town. These people had jobs because of their attitudes while pumping gasoline.

advance-ment

He also has advancement within his organization. The fellow that manages the place, Doug, started there when he was about sixteen. He's now about thirty-two. Another fellow who has been with him for more than twenty-two years. Although people do come and go, Bob says they come in planning to stay six months, and instead stay a year and a half. He says it's the way you treat them that gets them to stay. (Bob has one fellow who has left three times and is back again.)

Often in our businesses we feel that once somebody is working for us they shouldn't leave. But if there are better opportunities available, and if you open up those opportunities for people, the word is going to get out that your organization can be a training ground for people. The key is that the employees give 100 percent while they are working with you, and you give 100 percent back.

open up opportunities for people

Bob keeps track of his people and recognizes their personal and business accomplishments at the meetings. He does those kinds of things to show people what they can do with their lives if they really want to succeed. He has been known to hire people through counselors in the city of Victoria who work with young people with problems. If they seem to have the right attitude, they are sent to Bob, and he often hires them. He has had several people work with him who have come out of some pretty tough situations and turned their lives around.

keeping track of people

Another thing Bob does to keep his staff motivated, or as part of thanking them, is to have a big picnic in the summer. He also puts on a big event in the winter. He took me to one of the finest restaurants in Victoria during the Christmas season with all of his staff members—about thirty of them—plus another forty-five friends and relatives of the staff. He paid the full shot.

staff functions

While I was at this beautiful restaurant with all these young people I had a chance to talk to them and I asked them how they liked running to the pumps. Do you know what they said? "It's fantastic." One employee said, "You come in there some mornings, you're not feeling that great and all of a sudden somebody says, 'Up, get moving,' and across the parking lot you go. After you've run across that parking lot a couple of times you feel pretty good. We compete with each other. When we see a new customer come in, two of us get out of the starting blocks and head for that car just to watch the expressions on their faces."

a feeling of achievement

So there's your Herzberg theory. Bob's employees were motivated by recognition, responsibility, advancement, and achievement.

Team Commitment

For years Shell Canada wanted to hand out trophies and plaques to Bob. It wanted to fly him and his wife to Vancouver. Many times Bob has turned it down, asking the executives to get on a plane and come to Victoria to present it to his staff because, he said, "They're the people who are doing it."

Bob's employees have a "team code of commitment," which they put together themselves. If somebody is having a problem and their work is not done by the time their shift is over, everybody doesn't just walk out the door. They walk over and say, for instance, "Charlie, what can I do to help you get out of here quicker?" Often Charlie will say, "There's no problem. I've

team code of commitment

got it aced. Go home." But there are times when Charlie says, "Well, I have a ball game tonight that I'm supposed to be at. Yeah, I'd really appreciate it if you could give me a hand," and two or three people dig in and get it done and help him out. It's like when a goose is sick and two geese follow it down and spend time with it to see that it's okay until it gets back in the air.

openness and training pays off

Bob goes away for two months every year. While Bob is away, his business is run by Doug, the young manager, and by all the other young people. He doesn't worry about it at all, because the employees have ownership—they see the books, they have meetings every week, they set standards, and they provide super service to loyal customers. We talk about geese that can fly 71 percent further. Well, I see a service station that's flying 71 percent further because they all get in the updraft together and *move*. When you see one person run across the lot, then two people run across the lot, what do you do? You find yourself sprinting with them. That service station has the power of the V.

Dunsmuir is a role model

Bob was in an accident a number of years ago when he was on vacation in the United States. He was driving his motorcycle, and a man who was intoxicated hit him. For five months Bob literally didn't know his own name; it was seven months before he was able to walk into his little service station. But guess what? Everything was running in perfect condition. How many people reading this book right now who run businesses or manage departments could step out the door for lunch, not come back for seven months, and find the company running in tip-top shape afterward?

But could Bob Dunsmuir's business still be successful when put to the test? There was a gas war in Victoria a couple of years ago. The price of gasoline dropped to 16½ cents a liter.

What he did was call his staff together and say, "Do we really give super service?" They said they did. He said, "Well, let's see if we can prove it. Prices have dropped to 16½ cents a liter, and I don't want to play this time. Let's not drop our prices." They discussed it and decided they would drop their prices only to 41½ cents a liter—the price Bob paid for his gasoline.

be honest

They put a strategy together so that when customers drove in they would run up to the car and say, "Fill her up?" And people would say, "yes." The employees would say, "I just want to check to make sure you understand there is a gas war in town." Most people would say they knew that. The employees would then say, "But I also want to make sure you understand that you are about to pay 41½ cents a liter for gasoline here when you can go anywhere in town and get gasoline for 16½ cents a liter."

go the extra mile

The people would ask why. The employee would say, "We have decided not to participate this time. We want to find out whether or not super service really works, so we have dropped our prices to the price that Bob pays for the gasoline. So we are not making money on it, but we don't want to drop down to the 16½ cents with everybody else. We would understand if you did want to go to one of these other service stations and get gasoline for 16½ cents a liter. As a matter of fact, there is a service station a few blocks down the street that you can go to now if you'd like. But before you go, let's just hop in your car and vacuum your car out for you and wash your windows and go under the hood." They would immediately do this, and they lost very few customers.

A few months later I spoke to all the Texaco service stations for British Columbia and southern Alberta. As I was telling them this story a fellow from Texaco stood up and said, "I want you to know that I was at our retail gasoline association meeting in Victoria after the gas war was over. Guess who outvolumed every service station in Victoria during the gas war with his higher prices? Bob Dunsmuir."

So there is power in standing united. You can't give your customers good service unless you have a good team and good people focused on going in a certain direction—that is, flying in a V. Being united is so important that I have included twenty additional ways to help staff and management work better together.

1. Put together a ten-point team guide that everybody agrees upon. It could include things such as people picking up after themselves, no one destructively criticizing another member, and no one bringing his or her problems to work.
2. Compile a team list of small annoyances once a month. Work to correct them.
3. Have a bimonthly activity night (go to a concert, go bowling, etc.).
4. Have a team incentive and goal.
5. Acknowledge everyone's birthday.
6. Go away for a one- or two-day inexpensive retreat. It could be at a team member's cottage.
7. Set up a buddy system so that everyone has a support person. Change buddies every four months. Have buddy awards.
8. Encourage spontaneity and fun at work. Surprise each other.
9. Let different people take main leadership roles on a specific project.
10. Make sure that everybody keeps an individual identity and has individual space. This is important because in today's work world people are willing to be part of a team if their individuality is respected.
11. Complete personality profile assessment tools in small groups, and then talk openly about the strengths and weaknesses of each person. Have fun with it. Explain how it takes many types of people to make a team.

12. Have the entire team participate in a team-building course.
13. Have regular training on effective communication—how to listen so others will talk and how to talk so others will listen.
14. Include everyone in open brainstorming sessions.
15. Identify people who cause psychic pollution. Deal with the situation quickly.
16. Include others in the hiring process. People who have to work with that new person should have some input.
17. Hire friends and associates of some of your present top producers. Birds of a feather flock together.
18. Have regular meetings, and make them interesting. Have staff run these meetings every other week.
19. Pick a community project, and work on it as a team.
20. Provide opportunities for everybody to advance, achieve, take responsibility, be recognized, and do jobs they love to do.

Questions to ask yourself:

- What could I do to improve my hiring abilities?
- How can I acknowledge the work my employees do?
- What additional ways can we motivate our customers?
- Do my employees have the right attitude? How can I improve it?
- Could one of them take over my position successfully? Who? Why?
- Is my company united? If not, how could I improve in this area?

CHAPTER
NINE

The Royal Treatment

Just a little over a year ago, on Thanksgiving Day, I went to Charlottetown, Prince Edward Island. Before I left I sat down to have breakfast with my wife, Beverley. While we were eating, Beverley looked at me and said, "Bill, you look pretty low on energy and you've been this way for quite some time. You've been pushing yourself too hard. You used to take vitamins, and it was really good for you. Why don't you start on a new vitamin program now? It might help to get your energy level up." I agreed with her. So after breakfast I went over to the cupboard, reached into the back, picked up a handful of vitamins, knocked them back, threw a couple of vitamin bottles in my bag, and headed to the airport.

After I got on the plane, I started to feel a bit queasy. By the time I hit Ottawa they had the doctors on board trying to get me off the plane. That's how ill I was. But I refused to leave the plane. I had to get to Prince Edward Island for an engagement. They diagnosed me as having food poisoning. I listed everything I had eaten that day, and we traced my sickness back to the vitamins.

There I was trying to get healthy, and instead I got food poisoning from the vitamins. It turned out that it *had* been a long time since I had taken those vitamins—they were outdated by two years. The vitamins were rancid, and the handful I took did the job on my stomach.

People Remember Service

At about eleven o'clock that night I arrived in Charlottetown, was picked up at the airport by Ken McNeil (the business advisor for that area of our Newport program), and was driven to the hotel.

no food

As I was checking into the hotel, I told the front desk clerk how rough I was feeling. He acknowledged that I looked pretty bad. I explained to him that I had food poisoning but that I was starting to feel a little hungry. I knew that it was Thanksgiving and also that their restaurant was closed, but I asked him if there was any chance that someone could go into the kitchen and make me a turkey sandwich.

we have rules

"Not a chance," he said. "We have rules around here. The policy states that nobody is allowed in that kitchen except kitchen staff, and they have all left. Management has gone home, too. There is nobody here that can do it. I'd love to do something, but it's impossible." Ken McNeil said, "Bill, I'll go find you some food," and lucky for me Ken did. But as we were dragging my luggage into the hotel, I noticed the owner of the hotel walk through. The desk clerk didn't even try to stop him to see if it would be possible to get some food.

The next night I spoke to a full house and had a great evening. I went to bed at about midnight, but I had a little trouble sleeping. At about 2:00 A.M. I was asking myself, "Why can't I sleep?" It wasn't just jet lag. There was no air flowing in the room. I couldn't get any air. I picked up the telephone and called downstairs: "It's Mr. Gibson. I've got a little problem up here. I can't sleep. There's no air in the room."

"There's got to be," the desk clerk said. "You're talking to me." I laughed along with him because I liked his sense of humor. "Well, I really have got a problem because there is no air." He suggested that I turn the air conditioning on. "Just reach in by the closet and turn that little knob," he said. "It should come on." I went and turned the knob, but it didn't work. I phoned back downstairs and told him that nothing happened. "Something had to happen," he said. Then he realized that the air conditioning was off for some reason, so I asked him if he had any other suggestions. "Try opening the window," he said. Well, I tried the window, but it only opened a small amount.

is everything okay?

Needless to say, I didn't have a very good night's sleep. I got up at about 6:00 A.M., having only slept a half hour at the most. As I was checking out of the hotel the desk clerk asked me to check the bill. Then he asked me if everything was okay. I said, "No. I think $87 for a room that I couldn't sleep in is too much." He said, "Oh," and handed me the credit card slip to sign.

As I was getting into my cab to go to the airport I thought, "No way. I am going back in there, and I am going to speak to this young fellow and show him a chart that I use in my seminars." I went back in, and I said to him, "Let me show you something. It may help you on your job. I want to show you why most people don't come back to the average business."

handle my complaints

I told him that 1 percent of customers don't return to the average business because they die. (I think the death rate for *that* hotel was higher—no air.) Another 3 percent don't return because they move away. Another 5 percent don't return because of the influence of friends. Another 9 percent don't return because of the price. Another 14 percent don't return because of unadjusted complaints. I asked him if he knew what that meant. He wasn't sure. I explained that an unadjusted complaint occurs when he hands the bill to somebody and the person says, "I think $87 for a room I couldn't sleep in is too much," and he ignores the complaint and instead hands the customer the credit card slip to sign. Then he said, "Aaaah. You mean you might not come back." "That's right," I said.

give staff complaint authority

The majority of complaints aren't handled properly because the staff members are not sure what they are allowed to do when a situation comes up and the boss is not around to make the decision. When I asked the clerk if anybody had ever told him what he was allowed to do in a situation like the one he was in with me, he told me that nobody had. If you are a manager or an owner, you must have trustworthy staff members who know how to handle problems quickly and efficiently.

practice

To help eliminate unadjusted complaints, owners and managers should get together with staff members and make a list of the problems that come up on a regular basis, decide how these problems should be handled, and write down the solutions. Then test each other with complaints so that everyone knows how to handle various situations. This simple activity can reduce the business you lose.

attitude

Then I told the desk clerk that 68 percent of customers don't return because of the indifferent attitude of staff and management. I asked the young fellow to make sure that he let the manager and the hotel owner know about what had happened with me and told him that I would expect a call because I was going to be back there in three weeks to speak to the construction association. I told him that close to 500 people were going to be coming out to that session and that I was looking for a good story to tell, but if they handled this properly I probably wouldn't tell my story.

Compare that hotel to the one I am going to tell you about now. Seven years ago I was heading to a little place called Cornerbrook, Newfoundland, with my stage partner, Neil Godin. We were flying into Deer Lake from Halifax. Our seats were in separate sections of the plane—I was at the front, and Neil was at the back. The gentleman beside me asked where I was going. I told him Cornerbrook and he asked me if I would be staying at the Glynmill Inn. I didn't know. "You should hope you are," he said. "The place is famous for its great service."

positive rumors

As we were getting off the plane, Neil came and asked me where we were staying. He said that everybody at the back was talking about a place called the Glynmill Inn and that he hoped we were going to be staying there. I agreed with him. Later, when we were getting our rental car, the woman behind the counter asked us where we were going. I told her we were going to Cornerbrook. "Are you staying at the Glynmill Inn?" she asked. "I don't know, but we better be," I said. "It's a lovely place to stay. A real experience," she said. At that point I reached into my briefcase to see if we were lucky enough to be staying there. Lo and behold, my office had booked us into the Glynmill Inn.

anticipate what I would like

We arrived there around midnight. As Neil and I walked through the front door, the gentleman standing behind the counter looked at us and said, "You must be Mr. Gibson and Mr. Godin. You two have come a long way today." We answered, "We sure have." He then said, "Most people who come to Cornerbrook come a long way. When they arrive here it's usually around midnight and they're hungry. Unfortunately, the restaurant is closed. However, we don't like to see anybody go to bed on an empty stomach, so we keep sandwiches and pop here in the fridge, and there's coffee and tea, too. If you'd like a snack before you go to bed, we'd love to help you." He asked if we wanted chicken or turkey sandwiches.

My room was beautiful. I walked in and opened the window wide—there was lots of air flowing through my room. The next morning I woke up, got ready to go downstairs to have breakfast, and opened the door. I was lucky I had my clothes on because a maid was standing directly outside my door. She greeted me and asked me where I was from and if I had ever been to Cornerbrook before. "You're going to love Cornerbrook, dear," she said. "Let me tell you all about it." She told me all about Cornerbrook and all the places we could go and how lovely it was. She was a chatty lady with a beautiful personality.

help me pass the time

When I went downstairs to the lobby, Tourism Newfoundland was showing films on Newfoundland. In the restaurant I was greeted by a lovely elderly lady who led me to my seat. Within minutes I was served. Then she came back with a tray of magazines and offered me one. I thought I was on Air Canada. I had never had a magazine offered to me in a restaurant before. I looked at her and said, "Wow! The service is fantastic. How come?"

treat me like a guest in your home

"Well, let me tell you, my dear," she said. "About a year ago a guy named Mac took over the hotel. We were all afraid to death for our jobs. We thought for sure that we were all going to be fired. But Mac had a great meeting with us, and he said that none of us had to worry about our jobs here at the Inn. We only had to do one thing: treat every single customer who comes into this hotel as if they were guests in our own homes here in Newfoundland." That is exactly what they do, and if you've ever had the opportunity to be a guest in a Newfoundlander's home, you know the level of hospitality I'm talking about.

Think about it. In your own business, do you treat all your customers, whether they are in the store or on the phone or in a meeting with you, as if they were guests in your home? A down-to-earth philosophy like this can go a long way.

Resolving Service Problems

When I returned to Charlottetown three weeks later, I checked into a different hotel because no one had contacted me about my complaint. I spoke to the people who had hired me to speak and told them about the story I wanted to tell. They were a little nervous about it, but during the evening there were some problems with the temperature in the ballroom, the chairs were late arriving, and we had problems with the microphone. The person in charge of that session got a little frustrated with the hotel's service, and he gave me the go-ahead to tell the story.

it could be your business

So I told them the story about that hotel right there in their own ballroom. You can imagine the response I got. But then I asked the participants, "How many of you here at this session can see that this kind of problem could happen in your businesses?" Just about every hand went up. So in all fairness to this hotel, most businesses experience these types of problems. They are not so unusual.

I got back to Vancouver a few days later to find that I had had at least five phone calls from the manager and the owner of the hotel telling me that an unfortunate thing had happened. The young fellow had told them about the problem with me, and they had decided to do something about it. They had set aside a beautiful suite for me and put sandwiches in it and all kinds of other things. However, each thought the other was phoning me, and I was never contacted. They both assumed that I was going to stay in their hotel, but because I hadn't heard from them I checked into another one down the street.

react quickly

A little over a year later I was in Charlottetown again to speak for the Public Service Commission of Prince Edward Island. I went back to that hotel. When I checked in the desk clerk asked me my name. She said, "Oh, Mr. Gibson, it's so nice to see you. Your room's all ready. Let me get someone to help you with your luggage."

wow! a different place

When I went into the seminar room three staff members were following me around to make sure that the microphone and overhead projector were working and that everything was set up the way that I wanted it. We had a great session that afternoon.

When I went up to my room the phone rang. It was the young woman at the front desk phoning to make sure that I was comfortable in their hotel. I told her I was very comfortable. "I have one question for you, if you don't mind," she said. "Are you speaking anywhere tonight?" I told her that I had a short speech to make over in Summerside. "Would you like a turkey or chicken sandwich and a soft drink in your room when you get back?" I told her that I would love it.

When I returned from Summerside they had the sandwiches and the pop ready for me. The manager made sure that I was comfortable. He said, "Bill, there was a time when I was a little annoyed with you because of the feedback I was getting from that story about us that you tell. But you know, we needed to sharpen up. It's unfortunate that these things sometimes have to happen, but we get busy and miss the basics."

People in my sessions have told me that several years ago, when the hotel was still small, they were known for their customer service. People had gone through snowstorms and arrived there at three or four o'clock in the morning and found hot coffee in their rooms for them and a note to make sure that they were comfortable. Sometimes when we grow, the quality of service gets away from us and we have to bring it back in line.

You must react to situations quickly and follow through on them. Approximately 85 percent of the people will come back if you correct problems immediately and rise above their expectations. As a matter of fact, they become more loyal than somebody who had perfect service in the first place.

Until now I haven't mentioned the name of the hotel in Charlottetown because I didn't want to leave a negative association with its name. Now, however, these people have gone overboard to correct the situation, and I recommend the Charlottetown Hotel as well as the Glynmill Inn. Recently I had great coverage in Atlantic Canada newspapers, and the only person to send me a note of congratulations was Donnie, the manager of the Charlottetown Hotel in Charlottetown, Prince Edward Island.

Shopping Your Business

One of the things that I suggest to stay on top of your business is to shop your business regularly. Have a friend or a business associate pretend to be a customer for you to see how you are doing and give you informal or formal feedback.

pay for service results

Dunsmuir Shell has its pumps shopped every second month. Shell Canada is involved in it and puts up a bonus of $250 for good service, and Bob matches it for a total of $500. They shop one person on the pumps, and the employees never know who it's going to be. That person is graded. If he or she grades above a certain number, the $500 bonus is split between all the people on the pumps. If they don't make it, there is no money for anybody. How would you like to be the person that didn't make it and have to face the rest of your team?

This strategy gives you an outside view of your business and keeps you sharp. It is no different than a speaker like myself having evaluation forms to get feedback from the customers on what I'm doing and what they like and don't like about me and my programs. At the end of this book you will find an evaluation form. I would like your feedback, as a customer, on this book and what other topics you'd like to see me expand upon. In exchange for this information I will send you an audio tape of me performing "live." It is definitely worth the tape investment to have you on my mailing list for marketing my audio and video tapes, books, and seminars.

follow-up

You can also find out the quality of your service by calling your customers. Bridgeport Carpets, a multi-million-dollar retailer in western Canada, has set up a system in which an owner or manager phones all its customers after the carpet has been laid to see how happy they are with the carpet and with the people who installed it. If there's a problem, the key is in the follow-up.

Neil Godin and I were working with the people from Bridgeport Carpets, and Neil helped them to set up their system. He convinced Ron Bidewell, one of the owners, to get on the phone and talk to the clients to get things rolling. Like most business owners, Ron and his associates were a little concerned. Why phone customers if they are not phoning you? What if there *is* a problem? However, Neil convinced them that the phone calls would pay off for them.

let sleeping dogs lie?

The first woman Ron phoned began to cry when she found out that he was from Bridgeport. She was upset because the wrong carpet was laid in her home—a carpet worth several thousand dollars. Ron put the woman on hold and went searching for Neil—and you can imagine how happy he wasn't. He asked Neil, "What do I do?" Neil told Ron to tell her that Bridgeport would go to her home and take out the carpet and install a new one immediately. "Do you know what that's going to cost?" Ron asked. Neil said, "Trust me. It will make you money."

the customer is always right

So Ron apologized to the woman and calmed her down. He told her to come back to select another carpet. The irony of the situation was that she picked the exact same carpet.

Ron asked, "What should I do now?" Neil told him not to tell her the difference but to apologize for the other situation, take the carpet out, and lay it for her. So they did. They were very nice to her and went overboard to make her feel good—they even gave her a few extra things just to make her feel better. Within weeks that lady brought thousands and thousands of dollars worth of other customers to that store. The payoff was direct.

extra service pays

As I've said before, if your customers are unhappy and you correct the problem immediately and beyond their expectations, you are going to have much more loyal customers. So whenever you handle a complaint, or you have to give somebody a rebate or their money back, look at it as advertising. If you give someone $100 back and do it with a smile and appreciation, you'll get a great return on it. It's probably the best advertising that you can have.

chalk it up to advertising

Personalizing Service

Another important aspect of customer service is knowing the names of as many customers as you can. Whenever you are putting something through a cash register and you are using a credit card, look at the name on the card and call that person by name.

Several years ago, a hotel employee in Edmonton came up alongside me and said, "Good evening, Mr. Gibson. It's nice to see you." I said, "My gosh, you remembered my name. It was eight or nine months ago that I was here last, and it was six months before that. How did you remember it?" "Some people are easier to remember than others," he said.

my name sounds good to me

He took my luggage up to my room and called me Mr. Gibson several more times. As he was leaving the room I did something because I believe in shock treatment. I put my foot on the door behind me, slammed it real hard, stopped him, and said, "How did you know my name? Be honest." In a startled voice, he said, "Your name was on your briefcase, Mr. Gibson."

See, it didn't matter how he got my name—I was impressed by the fact that he called me by it. Simple things like that make all the difference.

keep track

Another way of personalizing service for your customers is to track their needs. Vicki Krotz, from the Scarboro Fair Store in Stratford, is now formalizing a system that will tell her exactly what her customers are buying so that when she goes to Montreal on a buying trip, she brings back exactly what her customers need. That's customer service.

Personalizing service does not always mean focusing on the key decision maker, because it is not always the key decision maker who makes the final decision. For example, children influence buying decisions in families. This is where indirect selling comes in.

put yourself in their shoes

Let's take a look at an example. Michael Vance tells a story about a dentist whose business wasn't doing very well, so he decided to go to a seminar on how to market more effectively. The seminar talked about marketing via children and focusing on that niche. When he came back from that seminar he and his secretary went through the office on their hands and knees, taking a child's view of their office. They got a feeling of what it was like to be a child at the dentist's office.

The first thing they noticed was that the guest desk was too high and the children who came in had to look up over the desk. They had the desk inset into the floor and put little chairs in the front of it so that the children could sit down and have eye contact with the receptionist. They even took the medical forms and made them simple so small children could help fill them out. Colorful graphics that educated children on caring for their teeth were placed on the wall and headphones were installed in the waiting room so that children could listen to stories and dental care tips on tapes. They built a play area for the children in the waiting room.

ask them

Then they did some research. After the children had their teeth examined, the receptionist would help them fill out a form on how they felt about their trip to the dentist. The most common complaint from the children was that they were terrified before the dentist did the work because they didn't know what he was going to do.

The dental staff did some brainstorming and decided to explain the process to the child before the staff actually did anything. The child would work on his or her own teeth without the instruments being turned on. This showed the child exactly what was going to happen, and it took away any anxiety. To top it off, on their way out the children received a signed photograph of their dentist to put on their wall—to keep the crows away.

Later on after the company grew, pictures of the dental assistants were put in the lobby so the children could choose the person they wanted to help them. The business in that dental office doubled.

Initiating an Effective System

To boost a business and keep it on top, you have to roll out the carpet and treat your customers royally. Here are some simple steps and points that will help you initiate a more effective customer service system.

1. Make a list of your pivot points. This is where contact is first made with customers. A few examples are
   - in the reception area
   - at the receiving and shipping dock
   - at time of delivery
   - at the phone order desk
   - during sales calls
   - during service calls
   - at the complaint desk
   - during community functions
   - at trade shows
   - in the store
   - while performing the service
   - by mail
2. At each pivot point, visualize and then construct what an ideal experience would be for the customer.
3. Brainstorm with your staff and associates. Compile a list of ideas and methods that could give the customer or client the ideal experience. For example, devise a list of complaints and how to handle them, or a list of twenty service standards that everyone commits to memory, or "mindblowers" performed at random that positively surprise clients.
4. Make a list of tools, skills, and resources to deliver your service. This could include customer service training, a budget for small gifts for clients, a system to record customer data, and so on.
5. Monitor the quality and effectiveness of your customer service system and give feedback. This motivates people because they can see how well they are doing.
6. Set up a file to keep track of service ideas and techniques that you read about, hear about, or experience. Offer awards for the best ideas brought in by staff that can be transferred to your business.

One exercise I sometimes get staff to do is to visualize who their customers are and what they are really doing for them. Let your imagination explore all the things you have been doing for people, their families, friends, coworkers, and the community at large. Plant that solidly in your mind and give unconditionally. The universal law says that it comes back tenfold.

Customer service opportunities are only limited by your creativity and how far you will go to serve. When you look at all the work that has to go into customer services, you may wonder whether it's worth it. When you read my final true story in this chapter, I think you will agree that it is worth it.

In 1973 a twenty-three-year-old man named Joe Kotow had a sales job working with a cemetery in Florida. One day he received a phone inquiry from an older couple who were interested in buying a mausoleum crypt. That night Joe made his way out to the neighborhood where they lived. At first glance it was obvious to Joe that this couple was not wealthy. It was not going to be easy to persuade them to buy a mausoleum crypt. The house was a $20,000, 1200-square-foot, two-bedroom home with one bathroom. The furniture was modest, and the couple was retired and living on social security.

This was an "old country" couple from Germany. While the husband did all the talking, his wife either spent her time in the kitchen or serving sweets and tea to the two men. The man obviously had an engineering background. He demanded answers to such questions as, "What is the stress per square inch the crypt could handle?"

Several hours later the husband would still not commit and said he'd call Joe if he decided to buy. The next day the man called and asked Joe to come and see him that night. He wanted to buy two of the crypts Joe had! Joe was surprised. He spent another evening with the couple and agreed to spread the payment over a period of sixty days. Joe could see that this couple had very few friends and relatives in Florida. When he was leaving he sincerely told them that if they needed anything, to please call him. He gave a business card to the husband and one to his wife.

Within a month Joe got a call from the husband. He asked Joe if he could hold his check for thirty days while he and his wife went to Germany. They needed the money. The company agreed to wait another thirty days.

Several weeks later Joe got a phone call from the wife in Germany. They were loading the car to head to the airport when her husband had a heart attack and died. She didn't know what to do, but she remembered the nice boy from the cemetery. Joe's business card was in her purse. She phoned him asking if he could help. Joe made several calls to Germany and arranged for the husband's body to be shipped back to Florida, prepaid. He attended the small funeral and didn't hear from the woman again until she phoned him one month later. She apologized for bothering him again, but she was in need of help. The trauma from her husband's death emotionally drained her, and she had ended up in the hospital for several weeks. She explained to Joe that she was feeling okay but that she was worried about the hospital bill, the two doctors' bills, and some other bills. She didn't even know how to write a check, wasn't sure if she had any money, and would like Joe to help her a little.

Joe went to her home and, with her approval, proceeded to rummage through her deceased husband's desk. He stumbled across a paid life insurance policy valued at $150,000. It also looked as if her husband had quite a few stocks. She had some money in the bank, so Joe agreed to take a day off work and go with her. They paid the bills at the hospital and two doctors' offices, and then he dropped her off at her attorney's office.

Joe waited patiently outside in the reception area while the elderly woman visited with her attorney. After quite some time the attorney approached Joe and invited him in. He told Joe that the lady explained to him all the things Joe had done for her. She felt that she never would have made it without him, and for his time and effort she wanted to pay him. Joe informed the attorney that he was not interested in being paid. He did it because he felt a responsibility and enjoyed helping her. The attorney then told Joe that the woman was quite wealthy. Joe quickly explained that he had seen her house and the insurance policy, and in his own opinion she only had enough to look after herself for several years. The attorney went on to explain that they had found an additional $500,000 paid life insurance policy and $2.5 million in stock.

The lady then pleaded with Joe, "Please take my gift. I have no children and no relatives anyway." Joe finally accepted the gift of 1,250 shares of AT&T preferred stock valued at $64,000 at that time. She also gave him $100 in cash to cover the cost and expenses for him taking the day off to drive her around. In addition, she asked him to accept a handmade crystal flower basket she had brought back from Germany. Joe still has it!

Every Easter morning Joe went by her condominium that overlooked the bay and picked her up and took her to the Easter Sunrise Service. She passed away a couple of years ago.

I met Joe Kotow in January of 1992. He had just been appointed CEO of Triple-A employment in Clearwater, Florida. Joe told me this story in the hospitality suite after I had just spoken to his office partners at a convention. Joe gave that elderly lady who was in need of a friend the royal treatment. He did it expecting no return, and look at the lesson he learned about giving and receiving.

The royal treatment does work—and not only with customers. It works with coworkers as well. During an advising visit with Royal Ford in Yorktown, Saskatchewan, I ran across a neat concept in manager-employee relations. Owners and managers would give employees "royal treatment" thank you cards for specific actions, such as putting extra effort into a task or improving a process. The idea was to treat people well—catch them doing something right and thank them for it. Happy, appreciated staff see to it that customers receive the royal treatment, too.

I'll end this royal treatment chapter the same way I end many of my customer service seminars. I've changed this slightly and I don't know who wrote it, but it says it all.

The Servant

Humility recognizes that the only master there is on earth is a servant. All those who seek to become masters usually fail. So few are seeking to become servants, and it is the servant whom others eventually call "master." This is true of everyone who at some time or other has been named master. The master is always working twenty hours a day while the disciple is sleeping eight hours and enjoying holidays.—Unknown

Questions to ask yourself:

- How can we get more repeat customers?
- What are ten service standards we should have?
- What are five complaints we get and how should we handle them?
- What companies and individuals do I consider to be the true masters because of their service? Why?

CHAPTER
TEN

Moving the Market

There are three key elements of marketing: (1) positioning, (2) strategy, and (3) creativity. Most people misunderstand these three basic concepts and make the mistake of buying the creativity first and then trying to set up their strategy and positioning. This is the wrong sequence. When you are talking about developing the advertising and promotion side of your business, you have to determine your positioning first.

positioning

What do I mean by positioning? Well, I'm sure that you have walked into a clothing store and left within a few minutes because you decided that it was not the place for you. That store was not geared to your type of personality, your economic situation, and so on. It was not positioned for you. Or you may walk into a restaurant and within a few minutes feel uncomfortable. However, that restaurant may be packed with people who are happy to be there because it feels comfortable for them. It has obviously positioned itself to attract a specific group of people and make them feel good. The restaurant would not be successful if it had you as a target customer with its present atmosphere.

To determine how you should position your business, the key questions to ask yourself are (1) Who are you positioning your business for? and (2) How do you position yourself to attract them?

demographics

psychographics

First you must determine everything you can about your potential customers. You must know their demographics—age, gender, living area, and income. You also must research their psychographics—that is, what they like to do. For example, you may have two groups of people in the same age range and with the same incomes. However, one group likes to barbecue in the backyard, drink beer, get together with friends, and go out to the lake; the other group likes to go out to beautiful restaurants, go to the theater, and drink fine wine. So demographics tell you *what* your potential customers are, and psychographics tell you *who* your potential customers are. Psychographics are often determined through reading habits, listening choices, viewing decisions, clothing, favorite places, hobbies, tastes in entertainment, and living area.

How do you position yourself to attract your target market? First, be sure your business location fits your target market. I know of a beautiful seafood restaurant that opened just one block too far down the street. The owner was from another city and assumed that the location was okay. The block he was on had prostitutes at night. He was used to that in the big city, but the conservative residents of this smaller town were not. They stayed away, and he went out of business.

It is also important to make sure that the advertising fits the people and that your services are appealing to them. The training of your staff, the sales approach you take, the character of your building, the inside of your office or store, and the promotional materials you use are all part of your positioning.

strategy

Once you have determined your positioning, lay out your strategy. What are you going to do to reach these people? Strategy is important. Many times small armies have defeated big armies. Likewise, small companies have grabbed major market share and over time have become number one. Strategy is often what makes the difference.

When determining a strategy, you must decide whether you're going to do defensive marketing, offensive marketing, blanket marketing, or commando marketing. Your size, ability, flexibility, and the amount of market you are dominating will determine which of these four basic marketing strategies you should use.

commando marketing

Commando marketing may be used if you are a small business or if you are a large company moving into a market that is strongly held by competitors. With this strategy you use innovative promotional ideas that are delivered literally in person. It could be that you and your team inundate a conference: take a suite, fly in 500 lobsters, and put on an excellent reception for clients. At the suite, your clients meet your technical and service people along with the marketing people. They all leave with a personalized gift and a piece of advertising in hand. Later you follow up with a phone call. This advertising is not public. It is more personal. You may not be able to go head to head with the competition, but you try to get a good toehold in the market before your competitors realize you are a threat.

offensive marketing

Offensive marketing is used if your business is a good size and is strong and innovative. You may be the attacker or the aggressor that keeps the big competitor on the defensive. Using offensive advertising and marketing, you decide on specific areas or times to try to dominate the market. Forty Winks Waterbeds did that and eventually became number one.

blanket marketing

Blanket marketing is used to cover the entire market. It requires a large advertising and marketing budget. If it is the best time of year for marketing, and if a good return on investment is possible, you may hit every conceivable medium that reaches your potential customers.

Defensive marketing allows a large company that dominates its market to defend its customer base. Knowledge and tracking of the competition is important when you are in this position. Sometimes your best defense is a good offense, especially if the attacker is showing signs of disorganization or weakness.

defensive marketing

Often a company may use a combination of these four marketing strategies. Large companies that are spread out over great distances usually have different branches at different stages of success. Some branches may be using commando marketing; the more established branches may use defensive marketing.

combine them

After you decide which marketing strategy suits you, determine whether the advertising is going to be television, radio, direct mail, billboard, newspaper, magazine, or a combination of these and other media. Once you know the positioning, you will know what radio stations your customers listen to, what television shows they watch, what newspapers and other publications they read, where they drive, what streets they live on, and what billboards are in their area. (There are statistics from ad agencies and media reps that can give you this up-to-date information.) Track the results of your marketing, and don't be afraid to make a change.

know your customers

Of course, you have to keep in mind how much money you have. Say you are aiming at thirty- to thirty-five-year-old males with above average income and you only have $5,000 to launch your product. You may do a survey in an upscale shopping center for that target group. You look for men between thirty and thirty-five years old and ask them to participate in the survey. The questions would focus around hobbies: what sports they play, what radio station they listen to, what clubs they belong to, what kinds of cars they drive, what magazines they read, where they shop, and so on. You use this information to select the specific ways to reach them. With $5,000 you may decide to cosponsor an event with a major clothier, a health club, or a magazine.

how do I reach them?

So now you have determined whom you want to reach and how you want to reach them. The third key element of marketing is creativity. You must design the creativity so that it fits the positioning and strategy.

The Importance of Frequency

In my opinion, the most effective element in advertising is frequency. If you reach 10,000 of the right people ten times rather than 100,000 people once, your advertising dollars will be much more productive. To obtain more frequency, run several commercials on the same television program or the same radio time block, on the same radio newscast every morning, or run several ads in the same newspaper on the same day. The key to

frequency pays

obtaining value from frequency is to increase impact by reaching the same consumer several times.

A one-time pizza commercial on a late night movie will have to be a great mouth-watering event to motivate a consumer to purchase. The same commercial run several times during the show can dramatically increase response. Even though you may reach a small number of people, if they are the right people and you reach them enough times with the right message to make them respond, and it is affordable, you have effective advertising.

In 1982 Terry Straker and I really blew the minds of the media reps in Calgary by buying two or three commercials for Forty Winks Waterbeds during one half-hour TV show. TV station personnel told us we'd still get the frequency we wanted by spreading the commercials out between programs that eighteen- to twenty-four-year-old males watch. But who was to guarantee that the same viewers watched all three programs? By placing the commercial in the specific TV show three times in half an hour, there was a much better chance to reach viewers two or three times and move them to action.

when reach is first

In most cases, the media would rather see you spread your advertising out. It gives them a chance to sell more clients into specific programs. A lot of their commercial packages are spread across time slots so that they can move their inventory more evenly. If you really spread out, you'll reach more people fewer times. There are times when you may want to do this. Maybe you are creating an awareness of a product or service just to back up a sales team. At a time like this, a widespread reach could be more important than frequency. The tighter you pull the scope of your advertising in, the fewer people you will reach—but you will reach them more times. Your reach depends on the budget. Go for frequency first, and then spread out to reach more people if you have the money to spend.

One way to build frequency is to repeat a specific point several times within a thirty- or sixty-second commercial or in a print ad or billboard. If a specific point hits you three times in a commercial and you hear the ad three times, that means you got that point nine times. Too many people try to do so many different things in their ads that they lose the impact of a specific message. (In Chapter 2 I mentioned that we spent a large portion of Terry Straker's advertising budget by the end of the first day of the campaign. Where possible, go heavy at the start so that the frequency has built and you get results on your first day.)

radio remotes

Remote broadcasts are another good way to use frequency. A remote broadcast is when the radio station goes out on location with a radio personality who does cut-ins "live" on the air. One of the reasons radio remotes are so effective is that the radio station may run four to six live cut-ins per hour. The heavy frequency moves the market. A remote announcer might be in your store and announce on the air, "Come out and visit us. I have two specials here in my hand right now. If you are driving up Hollywood Boulevard, turn right at Vine and you'll see me waving at you." It's an event with a show biz feel to it, and it adds frequency.

simulated remotes

You can also do simulated remotes that don't cost as much. A number of years ago, when I did simulated remotes with a two-location stereo shop, I would take two announcers, say Greg Lee and Randy Doule, and I'd put Greg in one store downtown and Randy in the Dartmouth store. They didn't actually go on air live, but in the morning before the event and for a few days leading up to it, the two announcers would talk to each other on prerecorded commercials. Greg would say to Randy, "Where are you going this weekend?" Randy would say, "I'm going to Kelly's Stereo Mart in Dartmouth." Greg would say, "Well, I'm going to be downtown, and we're going to sell more stereos than you will sell in Dartmouth." So Randy would say, "You think so, eh? Well you just watch. All the people that listen to me and like me are going to be out buying from me." And Greg would say, "Well this is going to be quite a competition. Okay, we'll find out on Saturday. Come down and support us."

On Saturday's commercials the announcers would say, "This is Greg and Randy, and right now we are down at Kelly's Stereo Mart stores. We've got unbelievable things happening here." We weren't actually live on the radio, but the day was an event. The sales were absolutely phenomenal.

create an event

Taking Advantage of the Media

radio is mobile

Radio can move the market. Remember that it's mobile—automobiles have radios. You also have a captive audience. So when I am going down the street and I hear a commercial that says there is a sale two blocks away, I can move.

the theatre of the mind

The power of the radio is that it is "the theater of the mind." You can create bigger pictures and concepts in the mind and do it much less expensively than you can with television. Radio has this tremendous power of imagination built into it. When you listen to the sound effects that go with good radio commercials, you create images in the mind.

What about television? Again, frequency is important. Today some of the TV stations do live remotes. For years merchants and promoters have been using remote radio broadcasts. It's a good way of promoting unique events, special sales, and store openings, and more and more businesspeople are adapting the concept for television.

John Gwynne-Timothy of Wood Motors Ford broke ground in Halifax with a series of five prime-time remote spots on CJCH television a number of years ago. The response was phenomenal—better than any other form of advertising they had used. The dealership reported that many excited customers had phoned to put particular vehicles on hold until they arrived in the showroom.

almost a TV remote

In Vancouver, Bridgeport Carpets modified the idea to keep production costs down. It produced a simulated TV remote with prefilmed commercials that featured an announcer in the store inviting customers to its seven-day marathon sale. The commercials were run frequently during the sale, and they had the same impact as a live remote broadcast, with a reduced ad budget. Sales for a seven-day event soared to over half a million dollars. Bridgeport attributed its success to the greater volume of traffic created by the TV spots.

local yokels work

With TV, creativity has to be powerful! But it doesn't have to be expensively produced. The home fuel division of Esso Home Comfort had local dealers go on TV and invite customers to do business with Esso. The dealer would say something like, "Hi everybody, this is Charlie Smith here. I'm your bulk fuel dealer," and then he would deliver the message. You knew he was reading from the prompter card, and he looked very awkward—he sure wasn't professional—but everybody in town liked him and said, "Hi Charlie, saw you on TV." The commercial worked because Charlie was happy and everybody thought, "Look at old Charlie speaking on television." It didn't bother them that he was unprofessional because they didn't expect him to be in the commercial in the first place.

watch your ego

A personality ad is effective—if you have a personality. If you don't, it just ends up being painful to watch. Often businessowners do their own personality ads if they don't have a big advertising budget. They want to stroke their own egos, so they do the television commercial themselves. Often it backfires because they don't have the personality or they don't look trustworthy.

hire a personality

Another alternative is to hire personalities. When I was working in radio, I would enlist announcers or talk show hosts to be spokespeople for some of my clients. You can do the same thing to endorse your business with television. Remember the American Express commercials? They are good examples of well-known people endorsing a service. The use of celebrities can give commercials definite power.

the power of TV

Of course, always keep in mind which medium is best for you. People sometimes use the wrong medium or the wrong tactics and techniques for their message. Television works better with certain products because you can demonstrate what it is you are selling or trying to explain. You don't have to create a picture in the mind; it is a form of proof for customers because seeing is believing. Therefore, it appeals more to logical or complicated products that need to be demonstrated. The thirty-minute infomercials you see on TV these days are excellent examples of the power of television in advertising.

newspapers

The power of print advertising is that people can read and reread it. If it is a complex item, you can use the words and a picture in the ad to explain it. It has a powerful frequency factor—you can look at the ad, and read it again, and again. You can also save it or tear it out and take it to the business it is advertising.

frequency in print

Print advertising has another frequency factor to it that very few advertising people understand and use. When Terry Straker and I were working together and tracking the advertising for Forty Winks Waterbeds, we found that we were getting $22 of sales for every dollar we were spending in the Calgary *Sun*. Now that's a fantastic ratio, compared with $10 for every dollar spent on the TV stations (by the way, that is also a good return), and $8 for every dollar on the radio station. We had spent $200 in the Calgary *Sun*, and we had $4,500 worth of sales back. We thought that it had to be a mistake, that it was a fluke to get that kind of return. But the following month the same thing happened again. The return was just phenomenal.

track the return

Another month we ran a full-page ad and had a 14:1 return on it—that's $14 for every dollar spent. Terry and I sat down and talked and we thought, "Wouldn't it be neat if we had another medium in town that could give us this kind of return? Nothing would stop us." Then we thought, what if we run two full-page ads in the same newspaper on the same day? If we are spending $2,000, let's spend $4,000 and buy two ads and see what the return will be. If we are spending $2,000 and getting 14:1 back, that means we are getting $28,000 for our investment. We were doubling our frequency. We wanted to spend $4,000 on two full pages to see what we would get back. The return only dropped from 14:1 to 12:1, which was absolutely phenomenal. We got $48,000 in sales for a $4,000 investment. From then on we used frequency in our newspaper ads.

You can even create frequency with two or three small ads. We used to run a couple of small but powerful ads that said, "Hey, big special on page 8. See it today. Waterbeds." Sometimes we used four little ads leading people to the full-page ad. You can do the same thing with magazine ads. Employ frequency when you use direct mail, newspapers, radio, and television. Several billboards along a certain route will also give you frequency.

Newspapers are put together using full-page spreads, so you could put half of the ad on page 8, for example, and the other half on page 56 and people would actually have to take the insert out of the paper to read the full advertisement. And if they didn't, they would still see half of the ad. They would see the other half when they got to that part and then they'd take it out. With the Calgary *Sun*, we had run so many single-page ads that after a while we needed to start doing different things. Sometimes we would even turn the ad and run it lengthwise so it became a broad sheet. Then if we wanted to, we could make a poster out of it for the windows. (By the way, poster your print ads around your business, run your commercials on your in-store sound system, and show your TV ad. It reinforces your message.)

Obtaining the Right Information

Too many businesspeople make assumptions or go by gut feelings when analyzing their market or determining advertising effectiveness. Today more than ever before, businesspeople need accurate information. Making important marketing decisions by guessing is too risky. You can obtain a wealth of necessary information about your market and your business by asking your customers one simple question: "How did you happen to hear about us?" Then you must record, analyze, and use these answers to your advantage.

A good time to record the answers is during the person-to-person contact when writing up the order. You can write the information down right on the invoice form. These records will form the basis of an important and valuable tracking system, allowing quick and easy correlating between sales, promotion costs, and individual media effectiveness. Ad tracking can help you generate maximum return on your advertising dollars. This in-house method for gathering information allows instant flexibility during personal consumer contact. It is also more accurate and costs less than hiring external sources.

Here are some factors that can be measured by asking the question, "How did you happen to hear about us?"

- the effectiveness of your media advertising
- the effectiveness of your signs and display windows
- repeat and referral business
- walk-in traffic

When writing up an order or invoice, keep track of the age and gender of your customers. Guess the customer's age. Record the age group. Use M, F, or C to designate male, female, or couple. All this information will help you develop more effective and profitable marketing and sales programs.

Use codes to register the responses to your questions: R for a repeat customer, REF for referral, YP for Yellow Pages, NP for newspaper, and so on. If your customer responded to a radio or TV ad, note the station call letters. Record the results of your tracking in a daily ledger, and summarize the totals under column headings every week or month.

By tracking you cannot be sold advertising; you buy it. You are the one who knows what works. My editor just commented that this only applies to retail. He is right if we don't bother to transfer the concept. I came to Greg through a referral from the Freelance Editors' Association. It cost him $35 for the listing in the directory, and with my contract alone his return could be as much as $500 for $1 invested. More than half of the freelance editors in his association do not believe that it is worth listing in the directory!

Note: You can blow your whole advertising budget if you don't keep your people on the floor in tune with your advertising campaign. Often the salespeople on the floor don't even know what's been in the newspaper ad or what promotion is on the air. A little thing such as informing your people can give extra backup support that makes advertising pay.

Directing Your Advertising

benefit statement

When you are designing your newspaper ads, remember that they are just like a story in a book. They have a beginning and an end. They should start with a benefit statement—for example, "Save 50% on Shoes," followed by the name of the business. If it is a product, a picture should follow. The statement should end with what action the customer must take, and it should include your business telephone number, address, and location, and a little map if you are hard to find. At least half of all newspaper ads have the business name and logo first rather than leading with what it is that they are trying to sell and what benefit it will be to the customer. Put the benefit statement first.

There are exceptions, however. For example, say that our organization moves into a community to market a program. If we did a poster drop or a flyer drop that has "Increase Your Sales" as the benefit statement, it could be more beneficial to put "The New Orleans Chamber of Commerce presents Increase Your Sales" because it carries such credibility. There are always exceptions to the rules.

The first objective of any direct mail piece should be to get attention. You want it to stand out from the rest of the material that's coming in. For example, my new mailer has a hologram of me on the front and a pop-up of me on the inside. It has such power and creativity that the chances of anybody throwing it away are very low. It gets circulated throughout the company that receives it.

go after the right person

Make sure the direct mail piece goes to the decision maker. Too often direct mail goes out to the company or the organization and ends up in the hands of the receptionist who shoves it aside as junk mail. Your direct mail has a better chance if it is addressed to the decision maker—the president or the purchasing officer. (Again, just like the personal sales call, it's after the fifth and sixth time that you hit everyone on the list that you will see the real return. The key is frequency.)

help customer reply

It is also important to include a business reply card or fax reply sheet. It makes it easy for the customer to get back to you. The card should be self-addressed and self-stamped. If you are mailing nationally or internationally, an 800 line is a good idea.

mailing lists

You can buy mailing lists from magazines, professional associations, other businesses, and mailing list houses. You can trade mailing lists with somebody who has targeted the same customers but is not selling the same products as you are.

newsletters

A newsletter also can be a powerful form of direct mail. For some businesses, newsletters are very appropriate. Recently I was speaking in Texas, and I talked about the *Royal Reporter* newsletter put out by the Royal Bank of Canada. Two people came up to me to say that they are receivers of that newsletter and love it. The Royal Bank profits from this informative piece of marketing.

direct mail

Know why you are using direct mail marketing. It may be just to get people ready for a phone call, or it may be to sell a product. The philosophy "keep it simple" is not necessarily true with direct mail. Some of the material that you get from American Express is five pages long. However, they know that if you are interested in the first few paragraphs, and if you are a possible client, you will read the whole thing.

Often you design your advertising according to how you would respond yourself. You might say, "Well, it wouldn't work with me, so therefore I am not going to do that." However, you might be really different than most buyers or the target audience that you're after. It's a tough call.

indirect mail

Flyers and mail drops are a little different from each other. Direct mail is stronger than a bulk drop because it is more focused. It's what I call extended personal marketing. It is addressed to you personally, and is signed. It is almost like a personal letter, and thus has more power than a flyer. A flyer drop involves dropping something unaddressed. One company recently sent out Lotto tickets to people via direct mail and informed the receivers that it would be phoning to let people know whether they won or not. A good percentage of the people that the company phoned took the telephone call, so it opened the door. That was the purpose. Another thing you can do is make your business part of an envelope with five or six other businesses. It's not as expensive, but you have to share the limelight.

double drop

An example of the double drop concept is when a pizza company takes a certain market of 20,000 homes and sends out 4,000 brochures to test the market—1,000 to each of four areas that cover the entire market. By tracking, it may find that two areas had an excellent return and the other two had a poor return. This is where I'd double drop. Hit the two good areas (total of 10,000 homes) twice in a week, and forget about the weak area. I have worked with people in fast food outfits that have had great success with double drops. We hit certain markets maybe every two weeks or once a month and then the slow area about every third month. We kept the awareness there in the slow market, but we didn't bother pushing it.

what day?

The amount of mail that you read is determined by how much is in the box. You will notice that a lot of flyers, supplements, and newspapers run Wednesday through Saturday because they are gearing up for the sales at the end of the week. If you are in a business that isn't driven by a weekend market, then pick Tuesday to advertise. People are back in their routine but are not swamped. In other words, if you sell business products you are more likely to get customers' attention on a slower, less stressful day.

fax it

The fax machine is another good way to market. You can fax a one-page ad for just a few cents and hook it up to a computer by installing a fax board. However, there are drawbacks. For example, faxing can get expensive if you use it during business hours when telephone charges are the most expensive. People get annoyed by junk mail tying up their fax machines. Also, you don't know how good the machine is at the other end—your faxed ad might end up looking bad because of a bad machine.

With direct mail, flyer drops, or just plain letters, the envelope can be important. The outside of your envelope is often the first encounter the consumer has with your business. An envelope can provide an excellent opportunity to communicate that special first impression. The number of letters and information mailed in a year makes the envelope a highly usable medium and a most valuable promotional tool to make a brief but important statement about your company. When you consider the amount of mail we all receive, it is important that the envelope create an "open me first" response. If your envelope has a junk mail look or does not project a feeling of importance or urgency, or is stamped with the words "bulk mail," the receiver may never get to your message inside.

the envelope, please

Do your envelopes really create interest or impress the consumer with a strong message? Is there something you could say about your business that would be more motivating than just your company name and address? Think about a productive message you could quickly express on your envelope. The extra printing and information frequency is free. Could you say something motivating about your company products or services? Has your business tirelessly served the community for twenty-five or fifty years or longer? Have you won some unique award or received some important recognition for special service to your community? Perhaps you are the top performer in your industry on a local or national level. Are your business and people providing some worthy public service in time, energy, or a financial way? Do you have a unique, one-of-a-kind product or service? Write about it on your envelope.

bigger can be better!

Another bulk mail product is the coupon. There are hundreds of the usual dollar-sized coupons stuffed in consumer mailboxes every month. These small coupons often end up tossed out, overlooked, forgotten, or buried under all the other paper in our lives. Why not try a giant coupon? Produce a coupon or voucher on an 8½-by-14-inch sheet of paper or even bigger. Bigger is better because it is less apt to be missed in a mail drop, and it will certainly attract more attention lying around the house or office. Be sure the coupon looks like a coupon and not a flyer or leaflet. Your offer should contain a strong benefit to the consumer and be printed with large lettering on both sides. Decorate with a coupon-style border to achieve that special coupon value look. If you really want to attract attention, silk-screen forty or fifty 3-foot coupons and hand-deliver them to customers who like being noticed. We all know people who like center stage, and this kind of customer will enjoy the fun and create a lot of interest dragging this coupon down the street to your store.

Or try a giant invitation to motivate a customer to utilize your services and products. The extra large proportions would certainly make the invited customer feel important, and the size would guarantee that the date wouldn't be forgotten.

Magazines are another way to advertise your business. Because of tremendous growth and change, the diverse nature and enormous variety in the magazine industry should cause every businessperson to seriously consider the precise target marketing advantage available through magazine advertising. National publications are of little value for smaller businesses in smaller centers. However, the large national magazines are now publishing zoned editions that allow smaller businesses to target within a smaller region while still enjoying the prestige of promoting in large circulation publications. This strategy has resulted in a greater targeting strength for magazines, as you can now choose specific occupation groups in any age level and target according to geographical area.

Aside from boosting target value, magazines are a more permanent print medium. They tend to stay around the home and office long past the week or month between issues. Many magazines become a permanent part of private and public libraries. The high-gloss paper and quality color reproduction of many publications provide the advertiser with a great opportunity to look its very best. Futhermore, over the years magazines have developed into an important and credible source of information. Consumers continue to turn to trusted magazines for help and advice on child-rearing, home management, consumer purchasing, and a host of business decisions.

it will move the market

Also don't overlook the potential of billboards or other outdoor advertising. The ultimate in outdoor advertising is the impact produced from the larger-than-life proportions of the billboard. However, the smaller varieties of sign-type outdoor media, such as miniboards and bus benches, also have market penetration.

In the great outdoors, large numbers of people can be reached very quickly as today's mobile consumer spends many hours a week driving the streets and highways. However, selective target marketing is more difficult and less accurate with outdoor advertising because the audience is constantly changing.

Some advertisers feel that the limit to the length of copy in outdoor advertising is too great a disadvantage to justify the cost. However, I contend that this is actually the major power in outdoor advertising, because the key result factor is the dramatic impact of short visual or verbal messages. Aside from rental space costs, the only other real expense consideration is the cost of changing graphics or copy, which rises with the more complex backlit billboards.

The types of businesspeople who use outdoor advertising are as varied as the medium itself. For some merchants, a billboard located close to the business will serve to remind the consumer to shop at its store while in the area. With the right message, a car dealer could use a billboard to convince a customer to drive 20 miles across town. A food store using a billboard, however, would have difficulty convincing a rushed shopper to drive that distance. Travelers and tourists on the road can be influenced to patronize restaurants, hotels, recreation, and amusement attractions while they are still hundreds of miles away! I have found outdoor advertising to be a reliable method of saturating a target market almost overnight and have used it extensively.

The promotional poster is an effective, low-cost, time-honored outdoor and indoor advertising communication. I can't think of any product or service that cannot be advertised with posters. Exhibitions, art shows, performers, and speakers use posters with great results. Some posters are so attractive that they become collectors' items.

Have you considered using posters to promote your business? Your posters, placed in the windows of banks, in retail outlets, or in any high-traffic area, could increase your store traffic. As in any visual medium, a poster can project the excitement and personality of your sales event. If you are promoting "The Greatest Show on Earth," for example, give your poster the visual flavor of an old-fashioned circus. Whatever the look of your posters, make sure they are appealing and easy to read. Be sure that the main benefit to the consumer is prominent, and don't forget the date, time, and place.

As an alternative to the more expensive professional variety, why not have your staff make your posters? A homemade poster, wherever it appears, helps to reinforce an image of low-cost, no-middle-person pricing. Handwritten posters are also much more personal, and in this commercial world, personal is appealing. You could even have small children do it. Put posters on bulletin boards at laundromats, in food stores, and at recreation centers. Posters could also be attached to your company vehicles.

The Message

Every year businesspeople pour enormous sums of money into ineffective advertising programs. Often the media is blamed for lack of results when, in fact, the unproductive outcome is ensured from the beginning. Creating the right message to promote the right benefit is often as important as choosing the right medium. Spend the time to determine the best message and the best way to present that message to the market.

An effective advertising message contains four elements: attention, interest, desire, and action. For maximum results, these four elements must then be wrapped in the packaging called "benefit to the consumer or buyer."

words work

In any print medium, the headline is crucial. The headline makes the main benefit statement and is responsible for the success or failure of most ads. It should be large—about one-third of the entire ad—dramatic, concise, and believable. The rest of the ad's verbal and visual message may be brilliant, but it will not be read if the headline does not demand and receive the reader's attention. Superlatives are effective: the biggest, the best, the greatest, the most, the fastest, the finest. Other phrases proven to be effective include the following: try before you buy, the seven secrets of, never before/never again, name your own terms, make an offer, opportunity knocks, absolutely free, enjoy the best, get the most, and discover.

Wherever possible, try to illustrate the benefit headline with copy and visual material in the rest of the ad. The headline and the copy below should always involve the reader's self-interest. Remember, after *I*, the most powerful word is *you*. Try to relate your message specifically to some personal concern of the reader, such as security, family, prosperity, health, self-image, career, comfort, leisure, or any other important human concern.

The copy should increase interest and amplify the benefit headline or statement by delivering the critical and motivating key information that details the product's advantages or benefits.

trigger my emotions

Emotional appeal created by copy or visual material can greatly expand consumer desire. For example, an ad for a heater might heighten interest in the product by expounding on the great economy of a wood-burning appliance, or by using a picture of a family enjoying an evening gathered around the heater. Imagine the flickering flames, the toasty warm feeling, the crackling happy sound of the fire.

Move the reader to act and react with important time-related details of your offer, such as the following: offer ends in ten days; supply limited; buy now with no down payment; no interest until next year; one cord of wood free for the first fifty customers. Try wherever possible to inspire the reader to take action—immediate action.

In a Yale University study, the following key words were identified as the most persuasive in advertising: save, money, you, new, help, results, easy, safety, love, discovery, proven, and guarantee. The power of your message is vital to getting a proper return on your advertising investment. Your message can move the market.

Don't be afraid to be unique. You will stand out. A furrier decided to develop a product line out of all the small fur pieces left over from coat alterations. He ran an ad with a phone number in the personal classified section of the newspaper that said, "Teeny, weeny mink bikinis for sale at itty, bitty prices." The response was phenomenal.

gossip sells

The classified ad section of the newspaper, particularly a personal column, is a well-read part of the paper. The personal classifieds can provide an excellent opportunity to create valuable, low-cost exposure, and it entertains at the same time. Imagine consumer reaction to an ad like this: "Dear Zelda, I can hardly wait to tell you what happened to me yesterday. I got into a sticky situation with Pam, but luckily it was resolved in next to no time. We were driving along the highway when I got a flat tire. This guy stopped to give me a hand, and he pointed out that both of my front tires were nearly bald. Well, wouldn't you know he worked at New Tread Tires. He invited me to drop in during their special Golden Days Sale. So Pam and I went down to New Tread, and the prices were absolutely incredible. I bought one steel-belted radial at their regular low price and a second one at 50 percent off—a savings of $26.95! And the service at New Tread was unbelievable. I barely had time to finish the complementary coffee and donut in their customer service lounge before they were finished. Zelda, I know you need new tires. Why don't you zip over to New Tread while their Golden Days Sale is still on? See you on the highway. Love, Fred."

Within a few days in the same personal classified section, a follow-up ad appeared. It was an enthusiastic reply from Zelda about her visit to New Tread Tires, with a vague reference to Pam. These exchanges continued for several weeks, and soon people were turning to the personal column as soon as they received the paper to find out what was happening between Fred and Zelda, the mysterious Pam, and New Tread Tires.

A tire store in Prince Edward Island tried this approach and became the talk of the town. A national TV network appreciated the creativity and ran it on the news as an interest story. The store's ingenuity produced thousands of dollars worth of publicity for a few dollars in classified advertising. I've had several clients try this with great success since then. Maybe you can use it.

tell more and sell more

Years ago a consumer may have been sold by a simple explanation of a product, but today people want and demand more details and diagrams. A fuller copy explanation or visual description of your product can make a big difference in helping to make your advertising work. One of my clients was promoting an excellent value by selling a $49.95 lady's purse for $29.95. The company designed an ad showing the use of the purse and boldly stressing the discount; however, the ad produced very little response. Together we worked out a new approach with a similar ad, but this time the picture showed the purse open, with all the inner compartments in view. Each compartment and pocket was tagged to describe the use—for lipstick, calculator, hairbrush, and so on.The extra explanation details made the difference, and the purses sold quickly.

"The more you tell the more you sell" is a good rule (with the right medium and providing you don't confuse the audience). The next time you run an ad, instead of simply discussing price or quality, give a full description of the product and stress the various functions. Price, quality, and appearance are important, but customers also like to know more about how products work before making a purchase decision.

Managing Your Budget

realistic advertising budget

There are almost as many advertising budget ideas as there are businesses. Some have an ad hoc budget, some have no advertising budget at all, and others spend what's left over after other expenses are covered. Still others spend the same as last year, on the same promotions, whether the ads worked or not. Or they create a budget based on what they think their competitors are spending. Carefully evaluate your advertising budget, and try to determine what is a realistic amount for you to invest. Too much is wasteful, and too little is dangerous. My suggestion is to create, not compete; determine your strengths, set your objectives, and then carefully plan your advertising strategy and expenditures.

Consider the following methods for budgeting your advertising:

percent of sales

- Ad budgets may be calculated as a percentage of sales based on last year's volume or next year's sales projections. Retail business and industry associations publish figures based on the average budget percentages used by various industries. However, these figures can be misleading.
  They are just average figures, and you must take into consideration that they include the good merchant and the bad, the big and the small, some who may spend "nothing" on advertising and some who spend more than they should. Use the industry average only as a guide. Contact the top six companies, find out their budgets, and work out the average. That average will be very useful.

task method

- Budgets may be created based on the marketing objectives known as the *task method*. To use this system, decide what goals are important, create an advertising plan to achieve those objectives without focusing on expenses, and then review the cost of the plan in relation to projected sales. If you feel that the budget is out of line, adjust up or down—either the advertising budget or projected sales. I prefer this method over the others. It is more realistic because it is based on identifying objectives or problems while keeping the freedom to adapt, rather than starting and staying with fixed limits. You can also determine what the main success ingredient in your campaign is and then cut the frills around it.

beyond break-even

- Some businesses require an even more flexible budget approach that more accurately reflects variations in business growth. If sales figures show that you are beyond your break-even point, then you may spend a much larger percentage to get those last more-profitable sales. For example, let's say that at one of my event seminars the break-even point is $20,000. Up to that point I may spend 25 percent of the gross on advertising. But once I break even, most of the incoming dollars are pure profit. Now I could spend up to 60 percent of the remaining volume on advertising and still make money.

- Some businesses budget a certain amount per unit that they expect to sell (for example, auto dealers).

Promotional Events

To close this chapter, let me give you examples of companies that have put advertising dollars into holding promotional events. Promotional events can move the market.

Sports on Broadway, a bar in New York City, does frequent promotions, a favorite being sports celebrity auctions. Well-known athletes auction off game balls, uniforms, and other valuable pieces of memorabilia. Fisher Nuts, a major nut corporation, is having a "sports nut of the year" contest at Sports on Broadway for the "nuttiest" fan. Cutty Sark also plans to sponsor a national Fantasy Basketball tournament in which fans will play one-on-one with a Hall of Fame basketball player.

These examples show creativity as well as a knowledge of positioning and strategy. Using these three concepts—positioning, strategy, and creativity—in the proper order can help you move the market.

Questions to ask yourself:

- What group of clientele is my business positioned for?
- What unique strategies and tie-ins can I use to reach the market more effectively?
- Whose creative work impresses me? Can I hire the same people?
- Who are the top producers in my industry that I don't compete with? Could I call them to find out the percentage of their budget they spend on advertising? Could we exchange ideas?

CHAPTER ELEVEN

Lean and Keen

enlighten-ment

On that 50-mile, six-day backpacking expedition on the famous West Coast Trail in British Columbia that I wrote about in Chapter 1, I experienced "en*lighten*ment." Being a rookie at backpacking, I wouldn't listen to my son Shane and my nephew Robyn Gibson at the time I was filling my pack for the journey. Extra sweaters, an extra pair of running shoes, lots of socks, special treats, my unique ground chair, and extra canned food didn't seem like much to me at the house. But 25 miles and three days later, crossing rope bridges, scaling up and down 300-foot canyons on wooden ladders, doing balancing acts on 30- to 100-foot slippery logs that span brooks and streams, and propelling myself across canyons on the two-seater cable cars, that extra 12 pounds felt like 50 pounds. Wisdom rules again; Shane and Robyn were correct!

a revelation

On the third day, I knew that somehow I must lighten the load. The amazing thing that happened was that I not only had a revelation, physically, in reference to carrying too much weight, but I also experienced a revelation about the load I'd been carrying in my business for the past three years. Business is much like backpacking. For short periods of time the extra load is okay, but over the long haul an unnecessary amount of overhead and frills can wear you down to the point of being noncompetitive. I am talking about being lean so you can stay keen.

check the weight regularly

During the good times and the turbulent times it is important to check the load continually to see that you are not carrying unnecessary extras. These extras can sneak up on you; it is like gaining weight. The West Coast experience whacked me on the side of the head and propelled me to action. I set a target to cut my unneeded extras and focused on a new direction that would eliminate hundreds of thousands of dollars of administrative and developmental costs. I also freed my mind for more enjoyable long-term projects.

Cutting the Fat

the lesson I forgot

Even though I had been taught about how to keep the load light, I forgot a few things. It's amazing how long it takes for us to learn our lessons in life. Five and a half years ago I decided to bring an investor partner into my company. This retired millionaire in his early fifties, who was previously one of my clients, had offered to get involved with me two years earlier. It happened when we were driving to a prairie town where I was speaking at a training meeting for his building supply franchise operation. At that time he told me that I was a great speaker, trainer, salesperson, and marketing pro, but I could use a few lessons on being a "real" entrepreneur, and after he retired, maybe he'd get involved and teach me.

I took him up on it two years later. After two short meetings he parted with an ample sum of money to help finance my growth and decided to come out of retirement to work a few days a week controlling the dollars, acting as an advisor to me, and overseeing our small but growing office.

Mr. Lean

I clearly remember the first day Irv Nelson arrived at the office. He was wearing a baseball cap, a pair of running shoes, casual slacks (wouldn't win a fashion show), a casual shirt, a jacket, and he carried his brown bag lunch in his hand. He immediately refused an office, even though he was 50 percent owner in the business. He said, "I'll share your office with you, and I don't need a desk. Just set up a table because I'll use your desk while you're away."

Irv had sold his share of the building supply operation and added money to what he already had. This man was worth several million dollars. He drove a small Toyota pickup truck, but most of the time he took the light rail transit to work. He has a nice home but nothing too elaborate, and he does not own a summer home or boat.

saving the pennies looks after the dollars

When he joined me he checked every invoice carefully, went for cash discounts, questioned prices, and was very cautious about adding unnecessary computer and bookkeeping systems. He disliked paying for my parking tickets or for unnecessary office supplies and equipment. He also didn't mince words (you learn that in the lumber yards) and was not sold on paying someone high wages in the beginning.

energy and time are money

Now you may be thinking that he sounds a little on the cheap side. There were times that I thought that myself, but after a few more years of business experience I have to admit, Irv was not cheap—he was lean and definitely keen. (I bought him out at a peak period. He sold high, and I bought high.) He was not afraid to spend money. He encouraged me to buy expensive clothes, saying "You need them, Bill. They are your working clothes. You are on stage, and you must look the part." He insisted that I fly executive class because of the amount of time I spend on cross-country plane flights. His reasoning was that my energy was my asset and I should protect it. He was okay with valet parking at the airport. Once again, it saved me time and energy. If my recordkeeping was astray on the product sales I did on the road (it happened often), he told the staff not to get upset. He'd say, "The money is here—just count the product and figure it out." He knew that I didn't need the hassles.

toys take time

You see, Irv respects time and energy. He doesn't own the summer home, the boat, and the recreational vehicle because he says it takes too much mental energy to think about looking after them. The more extras you have, the more you have to look after them. Every year Irv and his wife travel around the world for several weeks. He believes you should do it while you are young enough to enjoy it. People who have met Irv and his wife while traveling say that the Nelsons were a barrel of laughs and obviously he didn't mind spending when on vacation.

the baby boomers

Irv was born before the baby boomers, and his money management principles make a lot of sense in turbulent times and economic downturns. The baby boomer generation for the most part has lived a fast-paced, free-spending life-style that is inundated with big dreams and a collection of valuables and toys. With our new families on board, changing goals, and a challenging future, we are starting to view money and our time in a different way. According to my wife Beverley, "If you respect money, it will respect you." Her grandmother Newman taught her this—she ran a successful antique business called Hillside Antiques in Chester, Nova Scotia, until she was in her late seventies.

Cutting Staff

trim the fat, not the muscle

To be lean you may have to trim the fat, but make sure that you do *not* trim the muscle. That's where most companies make mistakes. They often trim the muscle and leave the fat. They will keep people (such as relatives or friends) who have been with them for years who are not really doing the job and not being productive because they feel obligated to them. Then they will cut someone who has only been around a year but who really does a good job. That person usually ends up working with the competition. You lose both ways.

In tough times it is heartbreaking to cut very loyal, long-standing employees, but it can be backbreaking to carry them. If you don't lay them off, chances are they will be gone shortly anyway because the financial status of your business will get worse and you will both be out of a job. I've had people leave in turbulent times and rejoin me eight months later after we made it through the situation. Start by cutting the least productive people on staff. Don't just cut everyone's hours equally—you need your most powerful people to pull you out of the tough times.

Sometimes we are unclear about what a real top performer looks like. There are top performers who intimidate and destroy teams, and there are top performers who support, lead, and pace teams. The kind of top performers you want in your company are like Wayne Gretzky—the Great One with the Los Angeles Kings hockey team. Wayne is a pacer; he helps the rest of the team perform better. He supports, he motivates, and he inspires the team. There are other star hockey players who do nothing but intimidate the rest of the team. You don't need people like that, especially during periods when you want everyone maximizing his or her energy.

the pacer

If you haven't got a pacer, get one. Or be one. During lean times in business it's time for you, the leader, to take a look at yourself and say, "I am really the pacer. I have to do all the things that the others need to see to make something happen for them. As a pacer, I must set a certain standard." The pacer is an important person who can make everyone else keen. Don't cut your pacer. I have some clients who have a different pacer each week. As part of the team, each person gets a turn to be be the pacer, to follow the team standards for a pacer and keep everyone else going.

When cutting and shuffling staff, this three-step process is useful: (1) calculate the exact number of work hours per week required to serve your present level of business in each department; (2) calculate the number of hours you, your partners, and the members of your families can contribute; (3) subtract step 2 from step 1. This represents the number of hours that you have to pay outside people for. Then select the best people for the projects.

Rather than laying off workers, explore other alternatives.You could turn a salaried sales and service staff group into an all-commission team or minimal draw plus commission. You could even trade staff with other businesses. For example, seasonal businesses can get together and arrange to swap staffs, (if one is busy in the winter and the other is busy in the summer). A ski resort and a summer resort that are not owned by the same people can work out an agreement. The ski resort people work in the summer resort and then the summer people can work at the ski resort, rather than both businesses looking for people who are already trained every season. They can even do joint training programs.

subcontract

You can also put your present people on contract. Contracting out is not just for external sales projects—it can be office work. There are companies that will carry payroll deductions and all the administrative costs of having people work for you. For instance, in the United States, Express Services have hundreds of offices. Bob Funk and Bill Stoller generated over

$200 million last year providing this service to U.S. businesses through their several hundred franchise outlets. Thinking lean doesn't mean cutting off your creativity. Take the time to be opportunity-oriented and you may be able to open up new horizons.

Being Honest with Your People

inform quickly

When you do let somebody go, it is important to communicate very, very quickly with the rest of the staff. Sit down and have a meeting about it. Inform your staff about what has happened and why, but don't get into a position of having to justify or defend your decision. Let the people know what is happening, and let them know what the future of the business looks like. Acknowledge that they are going to feel down and that they are losing a good friend, but immediately start some new plans of action and pull the team together. If you let it sit out there and drift, the situation can get worse and worse. It is very important for you to be honest with your people.

keep in touch

If you let somebody go, always make it known that you will pay them for any business they refer to you. You had to let them go because times were tough. That doesn't mean that they are absolutely lost to your business. Who else knows the business as well as somebody who has worked for you?

The biggest problem that most owners face is that they keep their troubles a secret and don't talk to their people. If you talk to the staff, you can get them involved. It's amazing what can come out of a good brainstorming session.

being honest and innovative

Nelson Building Supplies and Nelson Homes is a big unionized company in Lloydminster. When the company ran into some tight times, there was a meeting held for all the employees. Management explained the situation and opened up the books. All the employees looked at the books and voluntarily took a hefty cut in pay—everybody—to keep that company alive under less pressure. About four or five months later Mr. Nelson (not Irv Nelson) came up with a brilliant idea. Husky Oil was working on an oil-upgrader project (a surplus of heavy oil that they take and put through an upgrading process to get light oil), but they were short of accommodations for all the workers who were coming in. Mr. Nelson knew that in a year or so the local college was going to have a need for student dormitories, so he suggested that his company build the dorms for the college, paid for by Husky, which would be used as accommodations for all its people working on the upgrade for a year and a half. After that time, it would switch over to being the property of the local college for a student dormitory. It guaranteed work for his people and local contractors, plus he provided a community service. All of a sudden the company was back and moving. That's the type of creativity that is needed in tough times. For Mr. Nelson, being honest with the staff kept the company alive while it waited for a major payoff.

fire yourself

In the case of small businesses and some large ones, I've heard of managers who, when times were bad, laid themselves off. It is a tough decision to make, but think about it. Who is most employable in the business? If the business is running well but the volume of business is down, it might be better for the owner to find another opportunity rather than lose good people. Once the company rides the wave out, it still has its good people. This works especially well in smaller companies.

Business Strategies in Tough Times

it is not forever

If you are going to get lean, and there is a chance you may lose some good people, you have to remember that it's not going to be that way forever. If you are in a six-month financial dip, you may have to change your personal life-style so that you can keep the business and the good people you have. Look for ways to live and operate less expensively. You may have to stretch yourself if you are the owner or a highly paid executive.

the competitive edge

Tough times provide you with a great opportunity to hire good people. I talked to a fellow at a seminar who hired one of his best staff members from a competitor because the competitor was hurting and cutting back. Because the staff member felt unsure of his future in the company, he was willing to work somewhere else. Remember, a good staff member can increase business. You gain an asset, and the competition loses one. It can create a marginal difference.

train and develop

A down point in the cycle is the best time to keep your staff keen—that is, to accelerate the training and development of your staff. If you are ever going to invest the time, invest it now. Pull your team together and brainstorm. Let the staff help you make things happen. Set out some implementation plans and get them involved. Get them excited.

take advantage of the ebb

Most people think that they better not spend any money on training when business is slow because they might be increasing their expenses. Wrong. When things are slower you have the time to train properly. (It is also a great time to develop customer relationships.)

Before you make any decisions to cut staff, contact your local employment office and explain your situation. There may be some creative ways that you can go about this task. The government may even assist and pay half the wages if you keep the person employed. (It happens in Canada with Canada Employment and Immigration, providing that certain criteria are met.)

cut hours not jobs

Another strategy for staying lean and keen is job sharing. You can try to get your people to cut down the hours they work rather than losing their jobs. If it's only for a short period of time, you can cut them down to four rather than five days a week. Or you can consider loaning an employee or two to a community organization. In other words, if somebody in the business is not busy, but you want to keep them on, have them work only four days in the office (pay them for five) and volunteer their services out to the Kiwanis Club or somewhere like that to do community work. The business will come back to you. It's a great way to network and to advertise. Put the day's wages under advertising.

get mobile

One of the best things that people who are out of work can do is volunteer their time to a charitable organization. This helps them feel useful, keeps them busy, and gives them contacts. Because they are active, things begin to happen. This also applies to business. If your market has really slowed, go find something else to do that will make you feel good because you will magnetize business toward you. Don't hibernate just because it's winter; clean the closet.

check out the alternatives

Generally, if owners go through a change in their business and they have to let go of some of the staff, they will spread the change over six months because they are afraid of the impact it might make. If there is a lot of work in progress and projects have to be completed, it makes sense. But in most scenarios, executives don't want to make too much noise while they are making those changes. Personally, I say do it. Get it over with. Then you can start again; you can decide what you need to move forward. Do it in one move, but with advanced notice for the people who work for you. If you are going to be laying off staff, do your best to help them through the transition of relocating. Put them in touch with the proper government offices, supply references, and where it is possible help them find employment. If you are downsizing, find outside companies or government offices that run programs to make the transition easier on the employees. Consider how people are going to be affected and what it may do to the community and your reputation. Be prepared to deal with the media, the bank, and the suppliers.

To stay lean and keen during a time of transition, make sure that you have the round pegs in the round holes. Don't take your best salespeople and turn them into administrators. Utilize your remaining people to the best of their abilities. Don't be embarrassed to ask all your employees to hit the street and make you some money. Just sit down and tell them that it has to happen. Use their talents on the projects that they do best to give you the fastest results.

Often a move that you make in tight times can be profitable at a later date. Two years ago Despy Manufacturing sold its building for at least a 400 percent profit over what it paid for it. Now that there is a recession, the company has made an offer to buy the building back at the remaining mortgage. You can also do that with equipment and furniture. You can sell it, take the money, lease what you need, and pocket the extra cash for a rainy day. Some leasing companies will buy equipment from you and then lease it back.

down can be up— eventually

When cash is tight, most thinking needs to be for the short term. Change long-term deals into short-term deals. Determine which of your contracts would pay you up front for a discount. You may have a dream of long-term profits, but the reality is that if you don't have extra money in the next four or five months, you may not be there when the long term shows up.

money up front

Double selling of a complementary business is another lean and keen strategy. If you have a product that is not moving but can be complemented by somebody else's product or service, meet with that businessperson and develop a strategy to get your inventory out of the store. It could also mean doubling up at a location. This is not just cross-promotion. It's actually thinking about how your product or service matches or complements somebody else's who isn't a direct competitor.

double up

Making Wise Decisions

Often when we are on a roll we find that we're wasting a lot of energy on things that don't count. In business you are investing not only money but time and energy as well. To be lean and keen you must be a good decision maker. There are three things to consider when making a business decision: (1) time and energy, (2) money, and (3) reputation. Before you make a decision, ask yourself, "Do I have the time and energy to put into it?" "Do I have the money?" "Will it hurt or enhance my reputation?" "If I can't do it, who can?" Don't commit to a project until you have considerd three or four alternatives.

time, money, reputation

Determine what kind of return are you going to get for your time and energy, for your money, and for your reputation in the short term and in the long term. If things are tight, then the short term becomes awfully important. Remember, a lot of businesses lose in a downturn because they continue to think in the long term. They say, "Yes, but this won't hurt. Even though we are going to lose money, it will be good for our reputation." Well, if you lose any more money, you will have no reputation left. And the worst reputation is to be broke.

balance long and short term

When making a decision, line up three or four projects that are going to have the best return for your investment of time, energy, money, and reputation in the short term and the long term. Try to balance them. Then

be practical and logical

narrow it down to the project that is the most practical. Don't go for the ideas that are the most impractical. Sensationalism in the media leads us to believe that the wildest and the craziest ideas are the ones that make the money—that is simply not true. Although we see high-flying entrepreneurs hit the front pages of the media all the time, you will find thousands of millionaires who never hit the front pages. The most practical, consistent, steady, usable concepts delivered in an innovative way make the millions in business.

which gives the most service?

When all of the alternative projects seem to be equal in terms of time, effort, money, and reputation, ask yourself which will provide the most service to the community or to customers. The one that will give the most service is the best one to get involved in if the time, profit, reputation, picture, and practicality of the projects are equal.

prune your client list

Also decide which customers need the company focus. Consider pruning your customer list. Draft a priority list. Rate all of your customers A, B, C, D: A for very profitable clients; B for good profits and a possibility of becoming an A; C for fair profits but steady, with no possibility of becoming an A and only a slight possibility of becoming a B; and D for low volume and slow payments. Then you make sure that you are putting the right efforts into where you are putting your time, which is also your overhead. Remember 80 percent of your business comes from 20 percent of your customers. To be lean and keen, you must carefully review your customer base and the market you are after and make sure that your energies are invested in the right place. Have your entire sales staff do this along with your service and support group. You may find that a client is an A account for the sales department; but, the service and support groups may analyze the client as a D. Maybe you should consider dropping the account.

check your values

You do much better on projects you love or projects that satisfy your internal values system. When making a decision, lay out some personal characteristics or qualities that are important in your life and ask yourself whether they fit the project. For example, maybe freedom is most important to you. If you are down to the line and all other things are equal, it would probably be wise to choose the project that gives you the most freedom.

decision making is #1

Of all the attributes that help business succeed, the ability to make wise decisions is the most important. You may have a great sales organization and a good location, and you may train people well, but if you make a poor investment of time, money, and reputation, it could still sink you. On the other hand, I have also seen people who don't have exceptional talents but who are effective decision makers. They try not to waste their energy getting involved with people who could ruin their reputations. They avoid high-profile projects that waste time and become a big black hole that can drain all the money and all the profits from their pockets. People who just can't turn down a challenge end up with very little at the end. They get addicted and lose control.

Peter Thomas, an astute entrepreneur, invests only in business deals in which the upside is big and the downside is very low. He doesn't touch the 50/50 opportunities. He'll also give away 25 percent to someone who will completely handle the project. He says that, as an investor, giving away 25 percent to receive 75 percent of the profits is okay. He also establishes a minimum size for projects he personally gets involved with. He refers the smaller ones to associates.

intent and focus

A well-made decision is usually easy to implement because the decision maker doesn't waver. He or she goes for it and is committed. How fast you achieve something is defined by the level of your intent and focus—a good decision will give you intent and focus. You can't turn the powers of intent and focus loose if you are sitting there saying, "Well, I am not really sure which way to go. I am not sure if I want to do it." There's no intent. But when you seriously consider it, you end up saying, "This is a great decision. This is exactly what I want to do." With this kind of conviction, your wishes will come true.

urgency

Urgency increases the intent. Think how much focus you have when an emergency comes up that requires immediate attention. Compromise does the opposite. It dissipates the energy, disperses the power of the intent, and causes a loss of focus. Helplessness is the partner of compromise. When you believe that everything is beyond your control, there is a tendency to give up and compromise. In other words, you shrug your shoulders and say, "Why bother, it's no use" or "I'll give it a try but I'm not sure of the results."

Other Considerations on Staying Lean

Careful decision making, especially during difficult or unsettling times, can create energy and focus. This is being keen. Here are a few more considerations on staying lean.

people who cost less

- Consider employees who cost less. Companies often plateau, drop projects, change stages, and change direction. Over a period of time, the wages of some of your people may have built up to the point of being far above market value. Because you were making money (or thought you were), you gave raises freely. If these people do not want to take a pay cut (in line with the market) because of the changes, then lower-paid, well-qualified people may have to be their replacements.

temporary consultant

- Hire a temporary management consultant to help with the load when you are not sure how long a project will last. (Be careful that you don't end up setting up competitors and contracting your business away. I've done it, and it hurts. Have them sign noncompete clauses.)

save on benefits

- Take a look at ways to reduce employee benefits. Maybe there is a less expensive supplier of the benefits. Possibly you could combine with another business to get rates reduced.

be a horse trader

- Look for ways to trade off other services, benefits, and products for a reduction in wages. Maybe you can trade services with a ski mountain and then put a value on an annual pass for any employee. Or line up an associate to sell groceries wholesale to your people. Personally, you may have a car that you don't need and a staff member who needs one. These ideas would normally be used at a time when your back is really against the wall, but keep your mind open at all times. A dollar saved is as good as two dollars earned.

I want one too

- Be careful with buying one staff member a new desk, cellular phone, new computer, and so on. I bought two people cellular phones who were in the field, then everyone needed one. Those two cellular phones turned into ten cellular phones. Maybe a cellular phone could be an answer for increased productivity, but in my case, the majority would've bought them themselves. I made the mistake of buying the first two. Once you give someone a toy, it is hard to take it away.

save on phones

- Check out all the alternatives for long-distance services. Contact your telephone company regularly and review what you do. Companies often have new, less expensive services to offer, but they never tell you until you ask.

save with incentives

- Set up incentives for staff and management to save dollars for the company—but not at the expense of customer and internal relations.

In good times or bad we all need to have a lean and keen consciousness. It is smart business. But it is like anything else: if you overdo it, it doesn't work. There is a difference between losing a few pounds and starving yourself. Weigh your decisions carefully. Good staff and good customers are something to be cherished. Be creative before you lay off or prune.

As a small business operator, there is a story I tell about a small business somewhere in small town America. The inspectors from the Labor Board entered a small printer's operation in Small Town. They asked to speak to the owner. When the owner appeared, the inspectors told him that they had received complaints that he was underpaying his staff; they were there to investigate. They asked him, "Do you underpay your staff?" He said, "Definitely not." He admitted to the inspectors that he had five people working in the back. They proceeded to go there and complete five interviews.

The inspectors reappeared with disappointed looks on their faces. One of them said, "There is something wrong. All of these people are well paid. Are you sure there is no one else working for you?" He said, "Well, there is one more person." "Who?" replied the official. He said, "The Joe boy." "What does he do around here?" snapped the inspector. The owner said, "He sweeps the floor, picks up the garbage, does all the dirty jobs, and runs errands." "What do you pay him?" demanded the inspector. "He gets gas money, some pocket change, and a package of cigarettes now and again," answered the owner. "Where is he? Let me talk to him," instructed the inspector. The owner answered, "You *are* talking to him."

I'm sure that many of you are saying, "How true." In the next chapter we will focus on being "Financially Fit" so we don't have to be underpaid.

Questions to ask yourself:

- In what areas in my business or personal life am I carrying too much weight?
- Do I know someone who could be my mentor on being lean?
- What are ten comparison points that tell me which employees are productive and which ones are not?
- How could I use the concepts of (1) time and energy, (2) money, and (3) reputation to make a decision that I am wrestling with right now?
- How big of an upside and how small of a downside do I need in a business transaction?
- What is the minimum size of projects that I will personally take on?

CHAPTER
TWELVE

Financially Fit

Cash flow is tight, and you are doing everything you can to survive. The phone rings. A staff member answers it and says to you, "It's the bank calling." Within seconds your stress level skyrockets. You finally go to the phone and when you say hello, your bank manager says, "I've just phoned to wish you a good day. It is a pleasure having you as a customer."

Very few people have ever had an experience like that with a bank. As a matter of fact, I find that at least 80 percent of the business owners and executives at my sessions would like to have a different banker.

having the right banker

The right banker can definitely help you stay financially fit, especially during slow periods and while you're taking advantage of business opportunities. Here are seven steps to finding the right banker:

be a marketer

1. *Look at the exercise as a marketing effort.* Visualize the potential banker as a major client you want to make a sale to. Then develop an entire marketing strategy from start to finish. This will ensure that you are both physically and mentally prepared.

is the banker ready, willing, and able?

2. *Utilize your network.* Identify several potential bankers by contacting successful business associates, suppliers, friends, and friends of friends who are bank employees. You should also contact your accountant, lawyer, local economic developer, and manager of the Chamber of Commerce. After identifying the potential bank managers, gather information about them just like you would a potential client. Is the manager on the way up or on the way down? How old is he or she? Is this person active in community organizations? Which ones? Married or single? Children? Lives where? Which schools do the children go to? Does he or she participate in activities and sports? Is this person a risk taker or a "manager by the book"? Does he or she have large or small loan approval capabilities? The more you know, the easier it is to develop

a rapport by finding common denominators between the two of you.

3. *Set up an information-gathering, relationship-building meeting.* This should be done before making your formal application. At this session, you want the banker to do most of the talking. Ask questions such as the following: How long have you been with the bank? Where were you previously? Where are you originally from? How do you like the community? Where is the economy going? Bankers like to talk about themselves as much as we do. Remember that you are there to listen, gather information, and build a relationship. You are not there to sell—yet. Only sell when you are really prepared. You may only get one chance!

interview the banker

The ideal situation would be if a friend or client of the bank invited the manager to lunch in order to meet you or accompanied you to the bank. If this is not possible, try to get the friend or client to set the appointment for you. Eleven years ago I started my business with a $5,000 loan from the Toronto-Dominion Bank in Victoria, B.C. Mel Cooper is the owner of CFAX Radio and my previous employer. He vouched for me with Rick Batting, the bank manager. It took ten minutes to get the money. If you can't get a friend or client to do this for you, then make the call yourself.

At the beginning, let the banker know that you are there to gather information and get direction in order to make a formal application to receive a loan or credit line. Explain that you feel this is the best way to go about it so that it saves everyone time and energy. Ask what specific things he or she likes clients to do or not to do to make his or her job easier. Take notes—it shows that you are organized and mean business.

Let the banker know the approximate amount of money you are looking for. Inquire whether or not he or she has to go to someone else for approval. Some people dread going to their bosses. Often it may be obvious that you should ask for a couple of thousand dollars less than the banker's limit, to stay within their approval lines.

If the manager looks pressed for time, ask if you can come back at another time or get the rest of the information from someone else or on the phone. This shows respect for the manager's time. (As a matter of interest, several of the major banks have shifted more decision power to the managers in order to slim down regional and head office costs.)

strike while the iron is hot

4. *Immediately put your formal application plan together.* Strike while the iron is hot. Do what you have to do to gather, formulate, and present your case. Keep your business plan simple and understandable, but cover the full story of your past, present, and future. You are selling, so accentuate the positives and have logical answers to handle the opposing attributes. The plan should have the following:

what to include

(a) An overview or summary of your business.

(b) What the market is for your business and a flow chart of the activities you will implement to penetrate the market successfully.

(c) What your unique advantages are.

(d) Your soft spots and how you plan to offset them (this makes it real).

blow your own horn

(e) Amplification of the accomplishments, credentials, and experience of the owner, the board, key executives, and unique employees who are assets.

(f) Past and present financial statements with "explanations" attached to the statements.

(g) Projected future financial statements. Projecting three years ahead should be enough. If you do go beyond three years, explain the reality. It is more of a goal than an accurate projection.

(h) Cash flow projection for the next eighteen months to two years.

(i) A statement of your own personal worth and the worth of your spouse and other shareholders. (Get someone to help here. You may be worth more than you think.)

be realistic

(j) How much you need and why. Take the time to package this well. It may be the sale that vaults you to success. Be realistic about payments. If you are not realistic, the banker will not be happy later. You are only fooling yourself and setting yourself up for a poor relationship.

be practical

(k) Actual operational plans that banks don't normally see. For example, you may list things such as how you are increasing add-on sales this year, how you are improving staff morale, how you are using outdoor signs to stop the traffic, and how you train your staff. These are the things bankers never see that can give them the extra confidence to make a decision in your favor.

(l) A question-and-answer response sheet. List several questions a banker would ask and have a clear answer in the proposal.

(m) Promotional materials, press clippings, lists of awards, photographs, special achievements, reference letters, happy client comments, supplier letters, and industry data.

5. *Role play the meeting.* Role play the meeting in advance several times with an associate or family member. List all the objective questions the banker may have, and know the answers.

role play

6. *Remember that failure is part of success.* If you get turned down, ask the manager what you'd have to do differently to get the loan. If it is something you can correct in weeks, ask if he or she would be open to another discussion if you make the necessary changes. If the answer is no, politely ask why. You'll usually get the truth. Ask that banker who you should go to now or what you should change in your presentation with the next banker.

stick in there

Remember that there are federal, provincial, and state lenders, as well as venture capitalists and local economic development groups who may be able to help you. Don't overlook your employees. I've been in companies where employees bailed out the company.

other alternatives

7. *Realize that bankers are just people.* Bankers are just people trying to do the job to the best of their abilities. Relax, loosen up, and good luck!

stay loose

Once you have a good banker, take time to cultivate the relationship. Send the banker your achievements on a regular basis. Drop off articles and books that may help him or her on the job. Remember that a Christmas lunch, a small gift of thanks, or tickets to a ball game you can't use make someone feel appreciated and respected.

cultivate the relationship

Get your reports in on time. Late reports indicate slack, disorganized management or possible trouble being camouflaged. Try to keep the credit line moving up and down. Don't keep it at the maximum. You may be better off stretching a few suppliers so that your credit line stays down for a few weeks. If you get a balloon (e.g., increase of $80,000 on your credit line for one month), be sure to pay it when promised. It establishes a valuable track record.

be aware of danger signs

Keep your nose clean. Negative publicity doesn't excite bankers. Do you think Donald Trump's bankers and financiers ignored the Marla and Donald affair? I doubt it! We know our personal life should be our own business, but the fact is that it becomes many people's business if they have an investment in our future.

watch the publicity

keep good records

Keep good records and have a good system to keep the receivables in line. If you see a trouble spot ahead, go for the loan early. Last-minute requests show a sign of weak management or being overworked.

Managing Your Budget

Now let's see how we can operate our business so that we only need the bank to help us make money on that excess cash we've accumulated. If you are going to be financially fit you have to charge enough for your services or products. Bob Dunsmuir has close to the highest gasoline prices in Canada. I asked him why. He said that he figures out what kind of margin he needs per liter (or gallon) to give him the return he wants. Then he puts together a strategy that will make most customers want to pay that amount. This is a courageous attitude, and it works if you are willing to give the additional valuable services.

why you need margins

You need margins for a minimum of five reasons:

1. *Margins for profits.* Profits allow you to fulfill many of your financial and nonfinancial dreams.
2. *Margins for error.* You will make errors that cost money, and you have to have a cushion to handle it.
3. *Margins for competitive entry.* If you are the first to market a new product or service and have good margins, you can afford at a later date to advertise heavily, reduce prices, or add extra services or people to combat new competition. If you didn't plan for the competition, you may not be able to afford to tackle it.
4. *Margins for growth.* Research and development and the seizing of new opportunities cost money. If you don't have the money for this, you can fall behind in your industry.
5. *Margins for slow periods.* Economic downturns, unexpected interruptions, and seasonal slowdowns need to be considered.

what is a margin?

The margin is the difference between the real cost and the selling price. For example, the cost of an item is $12 plus 50 percent for fixed overheads ($6). The real cost is $18. If you sell the item for $24, your $6 margin accounts for profits and the other four reasons for margins. You use the same strategy if you are selling a service. For example, if you are selling twelve days of your consulting services, you would divide the twelve days of service into the total fixed overhead. For example, $24,000 overhead divided by twelve days of consulting equals $2,000 per day break-even before the variable costs such as materials for the project. Let's assume that the variable is $200 per day. The real break-even point is $2,200 per day if you deliver twelve consulting days. If you charge $3,000 per day, you have $800 per day to cover all the reasons you need margins. What if you underquote a job? (For example, someone going bankrupt and not paying a $6,000 bill.) What about extra travel you have to absorb? All of a sudden, you can see that the $800 per day margin may not be enough.

knowing costs gives you power

There are a dozen different ways to calculate your real costs, and each situation usually has several variables. Take the time to know your costs. That way you will feel more justified in asking for the right return on your investment. Knowing your costs helps you sell yourself on what you, your services, your people, and your products are really worth. Any accountant or experienced business owner or executive could help you in this area.

pricing tips

When pricing your product or service, test it to get customer input. Review the industry pricing standards and the competitors' pricing policies. Make sure that your price is consistent with your image. Know what you can discount and how far down you can go. Educate staff on which services or products they have room to negotiate on. Price certain products and services as loss leaders to build traffic and to bring in new customers.

discounting

Consider volume discounts and package prices. Know the psychological price breaks, and keep just below them. For example, rather than having a $5,000 per speech rate, I should charge either $4,800 or $5,600. You won't pay $5,000 if you have $4,200, but you might slip up to $4,800.

If you are a retail store, have all items priced. If you sell computers, services, or software, have published price lists and fee schedules. If you take trade-ins, consider it in your pricing. Automobile dealers often price slightly higher so they can give you good (perceived) value on a trade-in.

budgets and projections

Use budgets and projections to operate your business. Know your real break-even point. Review salaries, commissions, bonuses, and incentives, and budget realistically for them. Estimate yearly sales by the month. For real results, break sales down to weeks, days, even hours. Tracking makes it easier to see whether you are ahead or behind. Review the actual figures against the forecasted figures. What changes are occurring on the statements? What do these changes mean? Use an advertising budget book to track the results.

A few basics that you may want to have on checklists are the following:

1. Daily list: check the cash on hand, record all monies paid out, and balance sales summary sheet.
2. Weekly checklist: review accounts receivable (take action) and accounts payable (separate the ones that offer discounts from ones that don't). Take advantage of cash discounts. Even at 1 percent, when

interest rates are really low, it is worth it. On $500,000 worth of payables per year, a 2 percent discount gives you $10,000 for profit. It may require another $100,000 in sales to get that $10,000. Again, know your bank balance, make the contributions, and have payroll completed.

3. Monthly checklist: have statements available within ten days; review balance sheets; go over monthly accounts receivable, inventory, and new purchases and acquisitions; and do all monthly contributions.

For businesses with a good bookkeeper or accountant who does all these things, my suggestions may seem elementary. But my experience tells me that the majority of small business operators and accountants do not track and check this information.

controlling shrinkage

Another area that can affect your bottom line is shrinkage. Here are a few suggestions to control the shrinkage of inventory and supplies:

- Make sure that all invoices run consistently in order. This way discrepancies can be noticed quickly.
- Have anyone handling cash sign on and off. Have a supervisor or head cashier review all voids.
- Control and sign all discounts to make sure that someone isn't getting an undisclosed margin.
- Get receipts on all cash payments.
- Bank daily to avoid mix-ups.
- Post shoplifting and employee theft policies (if necessary), and be prepared to go the distance.
- Use nonremovable labels and tags.
- Make unscheduled inventory counts.
- In a service business such as a bank, make unscheduled calls to customers to verify balances and learn details. This is done on a random number of accounts. If fake loans are being made, the random approach will eventually make the problem surface.
- Check garbage bins. Occasionally you may find empty boxes that shouldn't be empty.
- Hire a shrinkage expert to "shrinkproof" your business.

insure yourself

There are millions of dollars of shrinkage in the country every year. It drives up the cost of our products and makes us noncompetitive at times. Don't think it can't happen to you. Bob Dunsmuir had a bookkeeper with a gambling problem who embezzled $60,000. He wasn't insured for that. He is now. Are you?

Squeezing the Checkbook

make money with money

Even though you are busy, make sure that you are earning money on excess cash you may have in the bank. When Irv Nelson worked with me, he was continually moving cash around to earn interest. He couldn't stand to see cash sitting in a bank account not earning money. The smarter you buy and the more you squeeze the checkbook, the bigger the profits.

shop around

Keep on top of how money is being spent, and try to curb any excess spending. Get several quotes, especially when things are tight either in your business or in the economy. You will be surprised at the difference in prices. Don't get quotes every time you buy something—just for the big things or multiple orders of small items. If it is over $300, call around; if it's under, why bother? You could be wasting time (time is money) that could be generating revenue.

put someone in charge

Of course, you don't purchase only big things—copiers, machinery, furniture, and so on. You also purchase paper, pens, paper clips, and felt markers that everyone needs. Usually someone starts saying, "I don't have a pen," and so 200 pens are ordered. The next month someone else says, "I don't have any pens," and another 200 pens are ordered. Put one person in charge of specific items. These little things do need to be ordered, but it's important to keep track of quantities. Use purchase orders, and have someone other than the person placing the order sign the purchase order.

Is that your best?

You should also consider how many suppliers you actually deal with. Sometimes you can make a deal with a stationery supplier for supplies that you use a lot of, such as paper and pens. The supplier may be able to get a special rate for you. A great question that you can generally use to get an immediate discount is, "Can you do better than that?" Most of the time they'll go lower. Or tell suppliers, "That is not low enough." They'll often come back with a better price. Shop around for suppliers, then stick with a few that can serve you best.

ask! ask! ask!

Often suppliers discount initially to get the business, but then the prices come back up as you give them more and more business. You have to keep checking prices. I'm not suggesting that you negotiate your suppliers to the point that they're not making money, because then their service quality drops, but if you don't ask for the discount you probably won't get it. It's just amazing who will give a discount if they are asked. Another thing you can say when phoning around is, "Instead of me phoning five other suppliers, I could give you the order right now if you give me an extra incentive." They'll often respond with a discount.

hang on to producers

However, remember that you get what you pay for. You might save a few dollars switching to another supplier or business, but you also might lose somebody who will work until midnight for you. I have a supplier,

John Hudson, of Lazer Data Graphics, who does work for me. I can call on a holiday weekend at the last minute, and he will go into his office and produce work that employees won't do. I pay a bit more, but I would rather stick with that individual than go somewhere and save a dollar. I make a bigger dollar with the work that he does.

better known doesn't always mean better

When you are searching for ways to save money while trying to get the job done, be careful. You don't have to go to the most expensive people on the block; you may be paying for image or a title. The results may be less with the high-profile person than with an unknown individual. For example, consider volunteer people to do window displays. Go to the local college that happens to have a merchandising display course for marketing students and give it an opportunity. In a number of the television commercials and window displays that Terry, Corrine, and I created and produced, we used students from the art college. We used our own props in the television commercials, and after they were finished we used them in our store. The price of having an art college come in and do the windows is negligible when compared with hiring a professional window dresser. We also used the students for market research. All community colleges have business courses for which the students need to do market research. Don't overlook retired businesspeople, mentally and physically challenged people, and senior citizens. I had a senior's fishing club help out with a trout fishing promotion at a mall for the department of fisheries in Victoria eight years ago, and they were great.

join together

You can also make joint buying agreements with another local business. If you are going to buy or lease a photocopier, do it together—especially if they are just next door. Consider forming a mini buying group with other local business owners. It is possible that you can work out a volume discount and buy together. You don't have to be in the same business. Split TV commercials, discounts on janitorial supplies, and so on.

are you really saving?

You must also be willing to reevaluate spending decisions. In some cases, there may be only the illusion of savings. For example, my organization was fooled by what we thought was inexpensive printing. We have had at times thirty-five to forty small training centers or training programs going on in various markets across the country. It only made sense to take certain items and get them all printed in Vancouver. But was it sensible? We had to box the printing and ship to each location. The cost in labor (lost opportunity time) and the price for shipping made it more expensive than printing locally at each office. We also had several calls on our toll-free line from each office. These people had to order, check on when it was coming, and so forth. That also cost money. When we switched to a local printer, it saved us money and also made us a better community supporter.

You must always be open to creative solutions to generate revenue. For example, you might have something you aren't using that you can lease or rent out. You can always share your office space. For example, when I first opened my office a few years ago, I looked at my office space and decided that I didn't need it all, so I rented out the boardroom and two other offices for $1,000 a month to Marilyn Lawrie, a businesswoman who was operating a job entry training program sponsored by the provincial government. The government gave her a budget for rent. I picked up $6,000, so it almost gave me one year's free rent, and she didn't have to worry about heavy long-term commitments. We both won.

sublet unused space

Auctions are another great way to save money, especially during recessions, when equipment, buildings, vehicles, and other items have been repossessed. Watch for auctions in the paper, and go to the auction houses. Norm Kilby, an advisor on an owner-development training program, saved tens of thousands of dollars for his clients. There were about thirty-five clients in his program, and Norm religiously checked the newspapers for any auctions in his area. One client he was advising needed printing equipment, and Norm spotted an auction that was selling a machine worth $20,000. His client got it for $3,500.

try auctions

You can also shop the banks for better rates if you have an excellent credit rating and good volume. When times are good, the banks are like most of us; they don't have to work hard for business. But when times are bad, they need the business, especially from good solid clients.

banks need business

You can also buy someone else's inventory. Try placing an ad stating that you will reduce other people's inventory for them. In other words, someone else might have a business that carries the kind of inventory you want to sell. You can help them reduce their inventory. It is best to advertise in another community. In tough times it is common to get inventory on consignment from a supplier if your business is solid. It is also possible that they'll give you several months to pay. A payment plan between the months of December and May, for example, is more attractive than having the inventory just sit in the warehouse at the manufacturer's location.

buy someone else's inventory

I have a client who went to a manufacturer and, being a good marketer, got not only inventory but also money to open more outlets. My client promised to go exclusively with that manufacturer and promised to pay the money back. The manufacturer had been dropped by a major retailer, which was my client's main competitor. My client phoned the manufacturer and said, "I hear that they have dropped you. You must be very upset with them." The manufacturer was upset and quickly agreed to get together with my client. Together they formed an alliance to take the other competitor on. The manufacturer put up the money, and both the retailer and manufacturer had great success.

use your supplier's money

form alliances

deposits

You can also save money by requiring your clients to put down a deposit for your product or service. People expect to pay deposits. It's usually just a matter of you explaining that deposits are customary in the industry. If someone is apprehensive, work with them to achieve a win/win agreement. If you are doing custom work, booking time for the project (consulting), providing products to risky clients or government departments that pay slowly, ask for a deposit. Deposits can really help your cash flow, but avoid relying on them to save you. Be sure that you could give refunds if circumstances demanded it.

Collecting Your Money

collect the money

So far we have focused on borrowing money, controlling budgets, reducing shrinkage, and buying more effectively. It is now time to look at collecting your money. A sale is not complete until the money is collected. You land a great account, you celebrate, then you throw yourself into the job 100 percent. Six months later, you still haven't been paid. A sale is not a sale until the money is in your bank account.

There are three objectives when it comes to collecting the money:

1. Get the money.
2. Preserve the self-esteem of your customer.
3. Keep the relationship intact.

get the money and keep the client

In most situations, you want to collect the money, but at the same time you do not want to put the other person down or negatively affect the relationship. Collecting is part of marketing. We spend a fortune to gain a new client, but a few wrong words on the phone by the accountant can cause you to lose that client.

First of all, you need to work hard at being a good communicator. Don't start off by accusing your client. "You owe me money, and you've broken your promise." A statement like this puts a client on the defensive. Try using "I" language instead of "you" language. You can say, "I'm in a predicament because I counted on the money coming in. Based on the promise that was made, I promised to pay my creditor and I am in a real jam because your check hasn't arrived. I am phoning you to see what's happening—help me." This approach will produce more empathy than the "you" message would.

use "I" language

A number of years ago I worked for a radio station in Alberta. There was an account that they had been trying to collect money from for about six months. I wrote an "I" language collection letter and explained the predicament I was in, the effect it had on me as the sales manager, the feelings it was leaving me with, and how it could affect the reputation of that company and how I didn't want that to happen. I ended the letter saying that I would greatly appreciate the cooperation of a phone call. I had the check for several thousand dollars in less than five days.

Also remember that the squeaky wheel does get the grease. Set up a pending system. If somebody promises to give a check by Friday morning and they don't, you can reach for that pending file Friday at noon and phone and say, "The check hasn't arrived, and I had been told that it would be here at noon."

squeak

There are two types of squeaky wheels: ones who use acceptable techniques, such as the one just described, and others who call two days after the invoice was sent and then call every couple of days after that until the bill is paid. Don't be the second type of squeaky wheel—you will lose your customers. However, some clients will put you into a position where you have to call them repeatedly. What you need to say to them is, "Look, I don't want to be phoning you back every two days making you not want to do business with me, so what's the best way for us to work this out?" There will be other times when people want you to phone them. They have so much on their mind that they appreciate the reminder. With permission, you can remind them. You could also say to them, "Write the check, give it to your accountant, and ask her to send it when your money arrives."

be courteous

Showing respect and appreciation is very important when collecting money. Anyone who owes any amount of money gets numerous letters that start with, "You promised to pay and you haven't." As soon as the person pays, especially if the letters are continually out in sixty or ninety days, he or she receives another similar collection letter. Instead of sending another "you" letter, try this. "I know how tight things are for you, and I want you to know that I appreciate that you made an extra effort and sent me the $500. Thanks for the consideration. Good luck. And keep up the effort." Think of how you feel when people phone, demanding that you pay. You dig, you scratch, you send the money in, and the next thing you know they are phoning for more money. So you scrape, dig, and send it, and on it goes. How much better would you feel if somebody called you to say thanks for the check? A little effort can make a big difference!

different strokes for different folks

It is also wise to treat different types of clients differently. Be flexible. Some people are very sensitive and are embarrassed if they owe money. If you phone them and hit them the wrong way, they might run and hide in a closet. There are other types of people, however, who are very thick-skinned, and it may be appropriate to get more direct with them. They'll often dicker with you.

state the terms

State your terms. One of the best ways to get your money after closing a business transaction is to immediately confirm the payment details. Then ask the client for a promise to pay accordingly. Even if it's only a verbal agreement, that person will find it uncomfortable not to follow through. If you make the sale without discussing payment terms or coming to an agreement, the client feels less obligated. Make sure that when the sale is made you state your terms very clearly.

check their credit

Get credit information on new accounts and accounts showing major changes in buying habits (perhaps they are into the takeoff stage). If you are going to get credit information, then use it. Often we don't want to hear the bad news about somebody's credit because it could ruin a good sale and the good feeling we had. Face the facts.

stay in touch

Also, be visible! As the sales manager and manager of radio stations for years, I would conduct sales meetings and always review the overdue accounts (thirty to 160 days) with the sales staff. When I asked a salesperson when he or she last saw that ninety-day client, he or she would answer, "The day I sold them the campaign." I would then ask how the program worked? The reply would be, "I don't think it worked. I haven't been back." Stay in touch. If people owe you money and you see them regularly, they are reminded that they owe you money. Drop by at every opportunity. Be in front of them. Frequent the social events they attend. Just by them seeing you, they'll feel pressure to pay or give an explanation.

keep them spending

Be aware that they may go somewhere else. When people owe you money, they are often so embarrassed that they go to your competition to get other work done. The key is to say, "I know what happens when people owe somebody money. They avoid the creditor and often use their cash to buy from a competitor in order to stay in business. That's a double hit if you do that to me because I am carrying you financially while you spend your money elsewhere."

You can work out a plan with the person so that what he or she owes you on a project doesn't have anything to do with the new project. Show confidence in the client. "I know you're going to make it, but I don't want to see you going to my competition because I need the revenue as well." You'll both understand each other's position and build a stronger business relationship. Work out a payment plan on the old bill, and treat the new purchase separately.

call off the dogs

If someone owes you money and they are being browbeaten by fifty creditors, you can sit down with that business owner and say, "Why don't we see if we can get all the creditors, including myself, to give you a break and not call you until the 25th?" You get on the phone and call the creditors on behalf of that person and say, "Look, she owes me several thousand dollars, and she owes you money, but we are all phoning her every day. We are driving her nuts. She is hiding from the phone. She's only working half the time. Why don't we all put it off and call from the 25th to the 30th of the month. She needs a break so she can get productive. I can get her to agree to answer the phones from the 25th to the 30th, but in the meantime she and her staff will be out making money so that there will be more around to pay all of us creditors."

use postdated checks

Postdated checks are also an excellent way to do business. All the time and effort you put into collecting money could be used to make money. So get postdated checks in advance. If somebody gives you a postdated check then and gets into a cash squeeze, that person is the one who has to phone and talk to you about it. People will remember that you are sitting there with a check that's ready to go through their bank. An interesting point about postdated checks is that in most states and provinces you can't sue if you accepted a postdated check that bounced. There was no money there when you took the check. Most people who would bounce a check would be embarrassed and would cover the check quickly. The few who may not cover it do not make it worth setting up a system of wasting hundreds of hours phoning and collecting because you are afraid to take postdated checks. Take postdated checks where possible even though you may lose a few. Also, if you have a client who is financially strapped and you have just collected a check from him, go to the bank and certify the check immediately.

use a courier

Use a courier, cab, or student for picking up money. Don't count on the post office! We wouldn't hesitate to spend $25 for a courier to send a proposal to get the business, but we allow clients to put the check in the mail. Tell clients this: "We have a policy to use the courier to deliver presentations to clients to get the business because we believe that speed is vital in the sales field. We've couriered you material before so you'd have it immediately. We have another standard here as well. We know that a sale doesn't mean anything until we have the money. We place equal importance on both getting the business and collecting the money. So we pick up money by courier or in person, especially checks of that size. There is no way that I want the post office handling a check worth $12,500. I would feel much better if a courier picked it up."

immediate follow up

They might reply that they actually don't have all the money. Ask them how much they do have, and then have the courier pick up the check. Don't just leave the bill unpaid because they don't have all the money. Accept what they do have, and keep track of how much they still owe you. It's important that they pay you something. Businesspeople often don't pay you the money they owe because they don't have the full amount. For example, they owe you $1,200 but they only have $700. Two days later someone they owe

$650 calls, and they pay it. Now there is no money. Call immediately, and you'll at least collect $700 of the $1,200.

barter your balance

Consider taking a service or item in trade as a last resort. However, be sure that there are no liens on the item. I know of a case in which an unemployed electrician owed money to a business. The business owner got the unemployed electrician to do a wiring job for a friend. With the permission of the electrician the friend paid the business owner. All three parties were happy.

Erasing Your Debt

last resort

On the other end, if you are in a deep financial bind and are having trouble meeting your financial obligations, here are a few last resort moves:

- Take short-term debts—such as revolving lines of credit, promissory notes, credit card balances, income taxes, and supplier balances—and try to get a consolidation loan. Spread the payment over three years. That will free up monthly capital and lower your monthly overhead. It will cost more in interest in the long run, but it may be what is needed in the present.
- Consider offering shares in your company to major creditors to wipe out all or part of the balance you owe. Have a good buy-back clause.
- Pay only interest payments for six months. Get special permission from the bank.
- Sell your receivables to a company that buys receivables. You will have to discount, but it may be worth it.
- If you have equity in your home or business premises, consider a second mortgage to pay off some of the debts. Pay the mortgage over three to five years.
- Consider a financially sound cosigner for a large consolidation loan. In return, you may put that person on your payroll for an agreed amount until the debt is paid.

put it into perspective

If all else fails, sell, sell, sell. If you owe $200,000 and have a decent cash flow, don't panic. Look at it this way—if you had to borrow $200,000 to stay afloat, you'd have real trouble. The truth is that you already have the $200,000 (you now owe it). It is simply a matter of scheduling payments that both you and the creditors can live with. Get the payments as low as possible with a commitment to increase the payments if things get better. I'm not suggesting that you misuse your creditors, but facts are facts. With good communication skills and a convincing plan of action, you will come out of it in time.

Questions to ask yourself:

- Am I satisfied with my banker?
- If not, then what are some things that I can do to find a better banker?
- If I am satisfied, what can I do to make the relationship even better?
- What additional financial tracking systems should I have?
- How can we reduce shrinkage in our business?
- How can we buy better and squeeze the checkbook?
- How could we become more effective at collecting money?

CHAPTER THIRTEEN

Mentally Fit

on vacation

The last piece of luggage was loaded in the car. We jammed the two boys and Tia Maria, our beautiful springer spaniel, into the back of the LTD station wagon. The Gibsons were now officially on vacation! As the car pointed north it began to rain. Bev and I looked at each other, silently saying, "I hope the weather is going to get better than this. We deserve an enjoyable vacation." Thirty minutes on the road in the middle of nowhere Ryan had to take a washroom break. Twenty miles later, Shane was thirsty. Not long after, the two boys began to fight. The two-and-a-half-hour drive to the borrowed condo was a strenuous one. When we got there, we were disappointed because the condo was half the size we had envisioned. There was no beach, and the resort didn't look too exciting. It was not what we expected.

making the best of it

Immediately, the boys seemed to get bored, and Beverley was on edge. I was trying to keep everybody happy, but I eventually started to lose my cool. Then all heck broke loose. Beverley let me know how frustrated and closed in she felt. The boys felt like there was no place to go and it was going to be a horrible holiday. "What are we doing here, Dad?" they kept saying. It was quite simple. A friend of mine in Duncan, B.C., by the name of Dick Drew knew that I needed a vacation and that I really couldn't afford to rent a condo. Dick arranged one for me at no charge. (My business was still in the survival stage, and there was not a lot of extra cash around.)

the meeting

I called a family meeting with a five-year-old, a seven-year-old, my wife, and the dog. "Let's look at what is really getting to us," I said. We discovered the problem. We had had relatives and friends continually visiting us for months, and Beverley was peopled out! She needed space for herself as well as time with me (I'd been on the road literally for months). The boys were upset that I was not going to get involved in many activities with them. They knew that Bev and I needed time together, but they wanted me, too. I, of course, was craving time with all of them. Does this sound familiar?

Balancing Your Time

You see, psychologically we all need a balance of three types of time: one-to-one time, group time, and alone time (see Figure 13.1). Whenever you feel off a notch, check to see how you are balancing these three types of time. If you are getting too much alone time, your system gets out of balance. You then need extra one-to-one time and maybe group time to even you out, and vice versa. Beverley had had far too much group time with the relatives and the children. She needed some alone time and one-to-one time. We realized that this was the problem.

balancing three types of time

I immediately suggested to Beverley she should go and visit a friend for a few days. This way she could get away from the crowded feeling of being with Ryan, Shane, and me. But she's a great mom, and she said, "No way." She'd feel guilty. With more support from the rest of us, she went for it. Her suitcase was already packed. We hopped into the car, drove back to Victoria, and put Beverley on a plane to Kelowna, B.C., where she spent a week with our friends Gordon and Lil Merry. She laid in the sun, read books, and caught up on alone time. She also squeezed in one-to-one time with Lil. The two boys and I spent a week of group time at the condo, swimming, fishing, playing games, and racing cars.

taking action

At the start of the second week the two boys and I joined Beverley and camped with the Merry's and their two daughters, Kiersten and Chelsey. We got more group time and spurts of one-to-one time. On Friday, Sharon Reid, my secretary, took the two boys, and Bev and I went for three beautiful days of one-to-one time. The balancing of the three types of time harmonized and refreshed our family.

refreshed

The key to balancing these three types of time is to have a list of the activities that you enjoy during each of these times. If you are prepared in advance to move quickly into fulfilling activities with each time state, you strengthen yourself mentally through proper use of your group, alone, and one-to-one time. I've provided my personal example in Figure 13.2. Use Figure 13.3 to create your own list.

what do you want to do

Reducing Anxieties

The subject of how to boost your business in any economy would not be complete without a chapter on being mentally fit. The power of the business lies in the mental fitness of the people operating the business. If 68 percent of customers don't come back because of the attitude of staff and management, we need at least one chapter on how to keep our spirits bright so that we can accomplish all the ideas suggested in the other chapters.

the need to be mentally fit

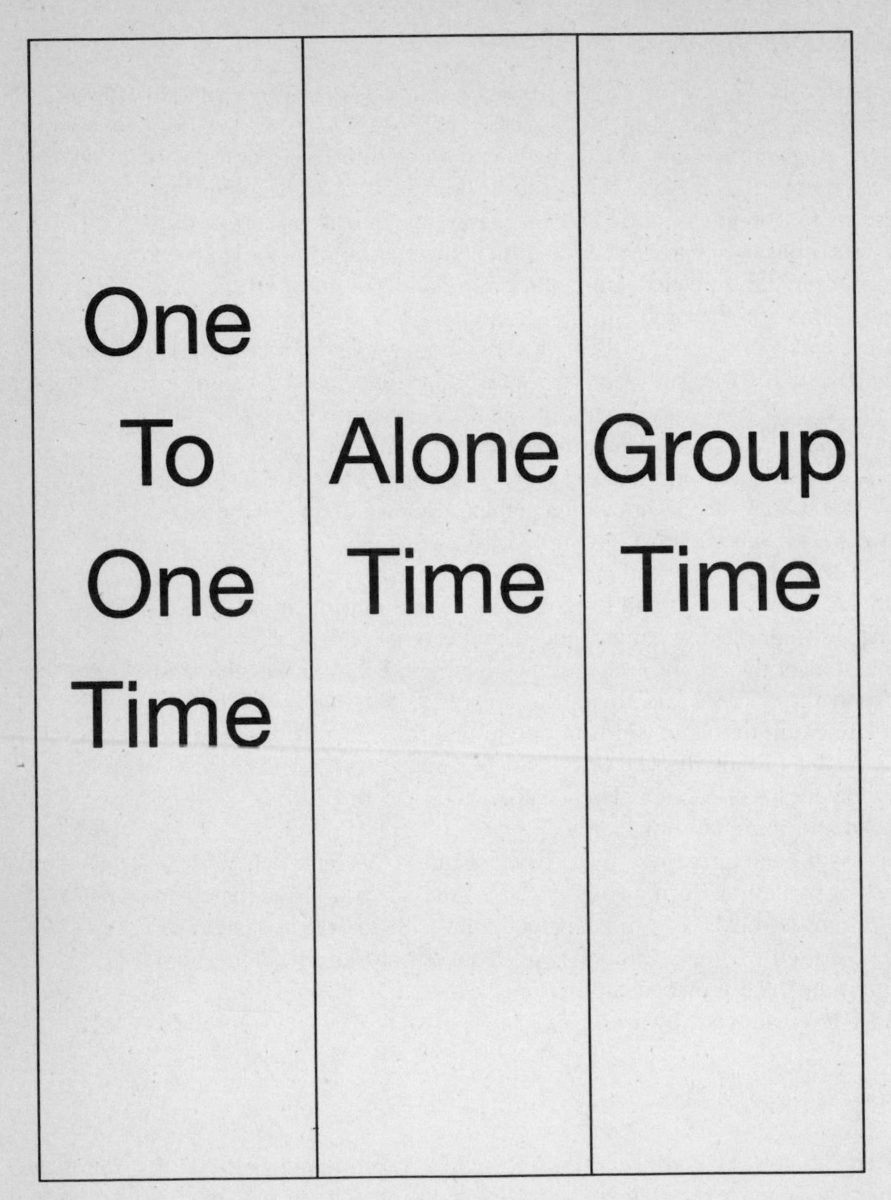

Figure 13.1

3 TYPES OF TIME		
One-To-One	**Alone**	**Group**
• Playing snooker and pool with the boys	• Listen to new age relaxation music	• Going to restaurants
• Laying in bed with Bev	• Browse through book stores	• Having friends in - fireplace, etc.
• Reading out loud with Bev	• Read spiritual and self-help books	• Talking philosophy
• Going to dinner with Bev	• Ride my mountain bike	• Brainstorming ideas
• Shopping with Bev	• Pump iron	• Attending seminars and conferences
• Fishing with Ryan	• Exercise	• Friday night at "Momma Godins"
• Hiking with Shane or Ryan	• Meditate	• Back packing
• Driving with a friend or business associate	• Listen to learning tapes	• Annual family reunion - Nova Scotia
	• Skiing	
	• Writing and creating	

Figure 13.2

3 TYPES OF TIME		
One-To-One	Alone	Group

Figure 13.3

There are people reading this book who have just gone bankrupt or are on the edge of financial disaster. Others are on a roll and are close to being out of control. There is stress, anxiety, frustration, and disappointment at every stage of business success and failure. But there are also challenges, rewards, excitement, fun, friendship, and opportunities at all these stages.

both sides of the sword

My goal for the remainder of this chapter is to give you quick, down-to-earth, tried and proven ways to keep yourself and others mentally fit, to handle the challenges, and to take advantage of the opportunities in these turbulent times.

the goal

You have no doubt had the experience of thinking of something that upsets you. Then another thought jumps in and says, "What about me?" and a third shouts, "Don't forget about me." Before you know it, your emotions are out of control and you are having trouble sorting out solutions for all these issues that keep bombarding you. Stop! There is a solution. Become productive! Once you become productive I'm sure that you'll start to notice the stress leaving.

becoming productive

When you find yourself getting upset, it is hardly ever because of one thing. It is usually a series of things whirling around inside you. Take control by pulling out a piece of paper or turning your computer on. Then move into the planning and organizing state, which is a productive mode. List every single large and small thought, issue, or situation that is bothering you. I'm talking about every one of them, including something someone is wearing that bothers you, a statement made by someone two years ago that is still upsetting you, a possible circumstance you are worried about that may happen tomorrow, and a regret you've been carrying for years. The key is to search and unload them all.

list it

What has happened? You have taken all of these issues out of your mind and put them on paper or in your computer. Now you can see them from a distance. You are less emotional.

being objective

What I'm going to share with you now is a very logical, simple method of reducing stress and anxiety. If you are stressed out about a few things right now, look at the sample worry and anxiety list in Figure 13.4 and use the worksheet in Figure 13.5 to complete a list of your own. Then follow me through the worry chart in Figure 13.6. Then come back later and cross off all the worries that are not real or those you can't do anything about.

the worry chart

Years ago I picked this worry chart off a tape voiced by the late Earl Nightingale. I've shared it with at least half a million people. It works! Let's review the issues that bother most people. Forty percent of those issues will probably never happen, at least not the way you think they will happen.

40% will never happen

WORRY & ANXIETY LIST

- Got to get "Opportunity Thinking" book & tapes to market fast
- Feel responsible for an upset general manager
- Spending too much money personally
- Bev's stomach bothering her
- Get Shane's truck fixed
- Getting "one night events" going immediately
- Not taking my vitamins
- When is Dale coming back so I can get computer disk?
- Anxiety over knowing exactly what to do to capitalize on opportunities: Nightingale Conant
- Will Ryan do OK in his tournament?

Figure 13.4

WORRY & ANXIETY LIST

- Your first one probably is what if someone sees this list.
  Solution: Use a blank sheet to create your own. Loosen up!

Figure 13.5

THE WORRY CHART

40%	Things that will never happen the way I think they will
30%	Already happened and I can't change them
12%	Needless worry about my health and the health of others
10%	Petty miscellaneous worries
8%	Real: Half you can't do anything about Half you can act on

Figure 13.6

Frequently we get ourselves uptight about what we *think* might happen. Say a couple is planning to take a vacation together, and he says, "Let's go to Hawaii." She answers, "What, and watch you gawk at everybody on the beach?" They haven't even phoned the travel agency yet, and a major problem is brewing.

be reasonable

In business, you might be in a tight cash situation and worried about what your suppliers are thinking. Have you phoned them and talked to them? Have you sat down with any of them and explained the situation? More often than not you haven't, so you have no idea whether they are upset or not. But rather than find out, you worry.

We can get caught up in the 40 percent of worries that will never happen the way we think they will. We create a whole lot of illusory problems in our minds that we don't need. So your first action on the worry list is to identify those things and tell yourself, "Hey, this is silly, they'll probably never happen." Write 40 percent beside each one that fits this description, laugh, and cross it off.

30% already happened and can't change

Another 30 percent of these worries have already happened, and you can't change it. This is the past—the mistakes you've made that you won't forgive yourself for. It is the guilt that you hold inside; the resentments or grudges you harbor. Remember that failure is not opposite to success; failure is part of success. In every failure is the seed of success. Ask yourself, "What are three positive things that can happen for me because of this situation?" The mind will always give you an answer. That is why it is so important to ask positive, result-seeking questions. If you say, "Boy, did I ever blow that, what a dumb person I am," the answer will be something like this: "You sure are dumb. Let me tell you two other areas you are a failure in. I don't even know why you get out of bed in the morning, you weakling."

second-try situations

In my *Exploring Business Opportunity* book, I talk about second-try situations and how you can find opportunities there. I can go into any community and, with the assistance of local people, make a list of all those businesses or concepts that have failed in the past and find an opportunity. The business might have failed for number of reasons: inexperienced owners; they could've been ahead of their time; maybe they were undercapitalized; possibly they knew very little about marketing; maybe they had a poor location. Just because that business failed doesn't mean that it won't work now. In your own business, it is a good idea to frequently review ideas and strategies that you've attempted in the past but failed at. Maybe today some of them will work. The past, like the future, is a great place to find opportunities.

Another area that causes stress but is something we can't change often is how we look. Some people spend a lifetime wishing they looked like someone else. The features that we were born with or that have been bestowed upon us accidentally are of the past and are quite permanent (for our earth stay). In most cases, we can only make minor changes with

the past

these features. Some people are tall; others are short; many have long noses; overweight people are common; some people are bald; others have big ears; some are too skinny. We are all unique in one way or another, and we are often identified by those unique features.

that's life

I have fairly big eyes, and they stick out. For many years I was very self-conscious about my eyes. I grew up in a small Nova Scotia community called Newport Station, Hants County, population almost 400 people. At the age of one I had a head the size of a large grapefruit, no hair on top, and eyes as big as they are now. Picture a set of adult eyes on a grapefruit. That was me. Fortunately, I eventually grew into those eyes.

it's a cruel, cruel world

Now in those days they didn't take "parent effectiveness training," and in 1946 my mother took a photograph of me at the age of one and wrote "Tweetie Bird" across the top. When I was four I picked up both the photograph and a Tweetie Bird comic book and finally got the picture of what I looked like.

Around the same time, my aunts from around the county would come to visit and innocently say things like, "Oh my gosh, look at the eyes on that little Billy. If you whacked him on the back of the head, they'd pop right out on the floor." And at that age, I didn't know how to hold them in. They'd sort of roll out and up when I looked at adults. At this point I began to be slightly embarrassed. I started school with very kind children; they nicknamed me Popeye. I got in wicked fights until I realized that it was just the big guys looking for a "live punching bag." I quickly stopped fighting.

everything is an asset

I came to the realization that anything can be an asset if viewed or used the right way. When I was thirteen, my friends and I started going to community and school dances. We would go into a dance at about 9:30 P.M., warm up for about two hours, and then make our way across the floor to ask a girl to dance. Just as we'd get there another fellow would ask her to dance. We would then do an inconspicuous pivot and go to the washroom (thinking no one saw what happened). We'd arrive back from the washroom and be greeted by our support group from the locker room. One fellow would say, "She saw you coming, and she beckoned him over." Another would say, "If you really want to dance go over and ask that girl over there. She'll dance with anyone." Off you'd go, knowing that she would dance with you. You'd ask, and she'd reply, "You've got to be kidding." In the middle of all the applause and laughter from your friends you'd make your way back across the floor. What memorable moments!

coming out a winner

I tell you this story for a reason. I didn't get turned down that anybody knew about. I'd wait until my friends had turned their backs, then I'd open these big eyes and project them out, home in on a girl across the hall (they could see my eyeballs at 100 yards in the dark), and with a gesture of my head and eyes, ask her to dance. If she said no thank you, I could just nod and smile, because no one else saw me get turned down. If she gave me the yes sign, I'd then say to my friends, "Hey guys, watch this. Let me show you how to get a dance." The girl always got up and danced, and my friends never knew the difference. I became a good dancer, and it probably helped me to be a more outgoing person as my self-esteem and confidence improved.

how will I remember you?

My point is that a feature I initially thought of as a hindrance eventually became an asset. Those big eyes enabled me to ask a girl to dance from all the way across the hall without risking the embarrasment of being publically turned down. Later in life, although many people meet me and forget my name, they will always say, "You know, the guy with the big eyeballs from Vancouver, Canada." That is positioning, that is identity, that is amplification.

who cares?

As you can see, I have a lot of fun with my eyes. Learn to laugh with yourself. Most of us would worry a whole lot less about what others think of us if we knew how seldom they did! Be proud of who you are. Take the time to be kind to yourself. You are unique.

At this point, go through your worry and anxiety list and cross off the ones that fit into the 30 percent category—those that have already happened and that you can't do anything about. Write 30 percent alongside those items. Think about the humorous side of these issues or the positive outcomes you've had or could have from these adversities.

12% are needless worries about health

Twelve percent of our worries are needless worries about health. "I slept near a draft last night. I think I'm catching a cold. By tomorrow my nose will be causing me a problem. By Friday it will affect my throat, and on Saturday I'll have a chest cold, then Sunday I'll come down with bronchial pneumonia. Maybe I should take the day off today, because Sunday is my normal day off and I don't want to catch bronchial pneumonia then."

Most of us spend far too much time worrying and complaining about needless health worries. You and I know lots of people you don't dare ask, "How are you today?" They will go on for an hour about their ailments. I do understand that there are some people who have real health problems, but for the most part our health problems are in our heads. Even when you do have a physical ailment, you can usually be grateful, especially when you meet someone with a bigger mental or physical challenge.

how much sleep do you need

One of the big health worries people have is not getting enough sleep. But how much sleep do you really need? Think about it. If the neighbor's dog keeps you up all night, you probably feel like saying, "I can't work today;

I didn't sleep a wink last night—I'm useless." But if friends you haven't seen in years arrive at your house at 11:00 P.M. at night, and you have a great time partying with them until 3:00 A.M. in the morning, chances are you'll have a great day the next day because of the great time you had the night before.

Often we get ourselves caught up in needing a certain amount of sleep; if we don't get it, we get uptight and have a rotten day because of our worry and mind-set rather than the actual lack of sleep. You don't need a lot of sleep if you have the right attitude. Just change your state of mind. (Continually getting no sleep *is* unhealthy!) Go back to your list and put 12 percent by those concerns that are needless worries about your health, sleep, or the health of someone else.

10% are petty miscellaneous issues

Petty miscellaneous issues, such as who squeezed the toothpaste tube in the center, who put the toilet paper on the roll upside down, or who took your pen account for 10 percent of our worries. These meaningless little things become major issues in homes and in businesses. You have undoubtedly heard it said before, but I'll say it again: Don't sweat over the small stuff. If you take that approach, it can make a big difference in your anxiety level. Cross off the petty issues from your list now.

Now, if you add up the 40 percent of things that won't happen, the 30 percent that have already happened, the 12 percent of health worries, and the 10 percent of petty things, you find that a total of 92 percent of most people's worries are not worth worrying about. That leaves just 8 percent of worries that are real concerns.

8% are real worries

Of that 8 percent, you'll find that half are things you cannot change. For example, it's a real concern if we are in an economic downturn or if taxes are raising all your supplier costs. But you can't change those things as far as the big picture is concerned. You may be very uptight because somebody you live with has certain personality traits that really bother you. But guess what? They're not going to change. You can either choose to deal with that person the way he or she really is or end the relationship, but don't destroy yourself because of the way that person acts. Maybe you should feel sorry for the individual instead.

Only 4 percent of your worries are real and unchangable. You simply have to learn to live with them. What items on your list belong in this category? Cross them off and figure out how you can isolate yourself from these worries or see them in a more positive way. Read the serenity prayer. It may help.

God grant me the serenity to accept the things I cannot change, the courage to change the things I can, and the wisdom to know the difference.

There is another 4 percent of real concerns that you can do something about. So when you've eliminated the things that are real concerns that you can't change, you are left with about 4 percent of your original worries. These are the things you can act on. The energy and time that we waste on the other 96 percent is absolutely phenomenal. What you need in turbulent times is energy and mind power. When we worry needlessly, our mind power and our energy are diluted—sometimes to the point of exhaustion.

the real ones—about 4%

Tackling Your Problems

The point of the worry chart is to give you a logical method that can help you stop worrying about the things that will never happen. Get rid of the things that have already happened, avoid needless worry about health, drop the petty miscellaneous issues, and cross off the things that you can't do anything about. Then you can focus on the real situations facing you that you can do something about. You can tackle these with extra energy now because you've dropped the rest of the energy drainers.

save it for later

Another way to tackle worries and anxiety is to consciously decide upon a worry time for the day. Then you say, "Okay, this is really bothering me, but I will write it down. I won't get into it now. I'll wait until six o'clock for my worry time." That way you can sit down and do all your worrying at once.

Some people may make a worry list once every couple of weeks. However often you do it, after a while you will see certain worries that keep cropping up. If these worries are there continually and haven't happened or are in the past, it is time to get honest with yourself. You are worrying about nothing. Laugh about it.

get busy

The worry chart is a great tool for keeping yourself in a positive mindset. It helps you to get rid of the concerns you can't tackle and pinpoint the ones you can. Then you can go out and do something about them. This way you become mentally fit. Even if you determine that your biggest concerns are ones that you can do nothing about, still do *something*. Get busy. If you're out of work, go out and volunteer while you're looking for a job. Get out of the house. Get involved with a volunteer organization. Once you get out there and meet people and give of yourself, you'll get productive feedback and start to feel good about who you are. You'll be surprised at the people and opportunities that come your way.

Anthony Robbins has an excellent set of tapes entitled "Personal Power." If you buy them and use them, I guarantee that he'll blast you out of inactivity with his state-of-mind-altering techniques. I've provided over 500 sets of these tapes to clients as part of the resource materials for one of our programs. They work!

If you are not enthusiastic, if you're sitting at home feeling bored and defeated, you can't expect somebody to come banging on your door shouting, "Fantastic! Have I got an opportunity for you!" It's not going to happen. The only way anything is going to happen is if you get out there in the middle of it and meet people, do things, and get advice and support.

You can also take action by starting an exercise program—it can reduce your stress. The only caution is to move into it slowly. Build up through aerobic exercise (but not at maximum) for several months, then hit the strength-building equipment. Over time you can change your metabolism. How much exercise? I don't mean that you should go out tomorrow and start jogging 10 miles a day and ruin your knees. But I do mean start moving. Maybe you just want to go for a walk; that's enough to start. Maybe it's a few sit-ups. But get started at something, and the rest will follow.

Dealing With Creditors

releasing the collection calls

One thing that keeps business owners or managers mentally down during tough times is getting phone calls every day from creditors asking for money. If you're trying to be mentally strong, to turn your business around, to make it happen, and every phone call is from somebody you owe money to, it makes your days very unpleasant. You find yourself making promises you can't keep because you don't want to say no—and that makes your self-esteem drop even more. You even tend to avoid being near a phone. Now you are really in trouble, and you end up in a downward spiral.

get productive

Here's what you do—use the strategy from Chapter 12. Call your creditors, or go visit them, and explain how counterproductive it is to have creditors calling every day. There won't be a creditor out there—at least, there will be very few—who won't agree with you that collection calls every day can keep a person down. Ask them, "How can I go out and make money to pay the creditors when I'm answering calls all day?" Then set a time that the creditors can all call, say, from the 25th of the month through the 28th. Tell them all, "I would like to get an agreement from you that nobody calls me between the first of the month and the 25th. During that period I will be a happy, fast-moving, productive businessperson who will take my staff out into the marketplace and maximize my opportunities so that I can make more money to pay you. Then when you call *after* the 25th I will have money and will divvy it up fairly to everybody."

Chances are that everyone will call you right on the 25th. You can be ready for them by then. If anyone breaks the agreement, remind them what you agreed upon and reinforce how well the system is working. This method of handling creditors is a way of setting it up so that you can avoid the negatives without pretending they're not out there.

Another way to deal with creditors is to set up buffers. If you have people in your organization who are really good at handling financial pressures, let them deal with the creditors until you are ready for them. Just become unavailable to take those kinds of calls at certain times of the month—instead, be out in the market making the money to pay them off.

Thinking Positive

see the positive

Another key to staying mentally fit is avoiding the negative and actively seeking the positive. Post good news items around the house, at work, or wherever. Have fun with it and share them with other people. When somebody says to you, "Hey, things are really bad," you say, "Is that right? Just look at a couple of clippings I have here." By putting good news around, you focus on energy building and avoid seeing the world as a totally negative place. When most people are feeling the blues, they tend to agree with everybody they meet that life is the pits. Find a friend, somebody you can talk to who can give you positive input.

hanging out in the right places

Remember that right now, while you are reading this, somewhere in your community there are people who are having the best days of their lives; there are also people out there having the worst days of their lives. Everybody isn't in the pits. If you go out and search for positive news, you can find it. Don't hang out in places where somebody is full of negativity. Go where you feel good. If this means avoiding your banker for a few days, do it.

mentors

There are many excellent books, tapes, and seminars that can help you change your state of mind and become productive under pressure. A seminar is often useful not only for the ideas it provides but also for the company you meet there. My marketing and training company and associates conduct a series of business owner development programs. Forty or fifty businesses in a community enroll, and over a period of eight to ten months they all meet for a series of seminars. They also receive on-site visits from an experienced business advisor plus small-group networking sessions for executives to sit down and discuss real issues.

Businesses that are in programs like ours very seldom feel the blues because they don't have a chance to stay down. If someone is down, he or she is brought up by the other people who are doing things. They have direct mentors who can assist them. (Indirect mentors are people you read or hear about.)

it got me

A year and a half ago, my company was tied into a federal government program that subsidized training for a lot of small businesses. Bill C-21, which was the legislation to provide small business assistance for much of this training, was held up in a one-year debate in the Canadian Senate. Many of the markets we had counted on opening were delayed after we had invested a fair amount of money in them, which created a bit of a recession for my company. So when, in addition to that, some of my key people stepped away and became competitors, I soon became mentally tapped. My energy was down, I was irritable, and I was caught up in the "us and them" thinking. I didn't want to trust anybody. I started to become immobilized. Procrastination began to set in. I was giving my power away by thinking, "They really ruined me." I was alternating between blaming myself and blaming others—all without doing anything.

make a move

What I did to turn myself around was to first recognize that I was down. When I realized that, I got together with Angeline, a friend of mine who specializes in self-talk tapes. We discussed a number of things that I thought were bothering me, personal and business. I spent two hours with Angeline, and she and I picked out the areas I needed to work on in terms of my self-esteem, my confidence, and my abilities as a leader. She then created "self-talk" statements. With the self-talk statements in hand, I actually went into a studio and recorded them. Over and above my voice we added New Age music and behind that a series of subliminal self-esteem-building messages.

set a time limit

I then sat down with my wife. I said, "In thirty days this whole situation will be drastically changed for the positive." We agreed that, for a set time, I would work like crazy. My family would be prepared for it. The kids would understand that I couldn't spend a lot of time with them on the weekends and that when I was around I might be in my office at the house, hard at work looking after the welfare of all of us. It's very important to notify the people close to you that something has to happen.

I listened to my tape at least an hour a day—on planes, in my car, late at night before I went to bed, and early in the morning when I first woke up. I also started listening to tapes by other speakers. I found several on enthusiasm that were really exciting. The tapes made me realize how important it is to be enthusiastic. Have you ever seen an enthusiastic failure? Enthusiasm drives you forward.

I also made a list of all the things that were bothering me and ran it through the worry chart. I identified which worries I was wasting time on and which ones were worth tackling. Then I moved into action, making the necessary contacts on the road to recovery.

be grateful

I also made a list of what I really had going for me, business and personal. I had been thinking that the world was falling apart. I thought I had been short-changed, that nothing had gone right, that I was a victim. I had lost sight of all the things I had. So I started building the list of things that I should be grateful for. I said to myself, "I have one of the finest life partners that anybody could ever want—my wife, Beverley." I realized then that, even if that relationship were all I had, I'd still have a lot.

Then there were the two children, my good health, the fine business that I had developed, and the reputation and name that I had across the country. I started making a list of all the good people I still had around me: Terry Straker, Rick Gibson-Shaw, Mike Pals, Peter Grey, Bob Davidson, Dennis Cauvier, Tim and Steve Maloney, and many more.

pamper yourself

Instead of focusing on the few things I didn't have, I looked at what I had going for me and I began to gain power. I began to feel good about myself. All this was reinforced by my tape continually saying things such as "Bill, you're a powerful leader. You trust your intuition, and you move quickly." Well, intuitively I knew that specifics were not going right in my business but I had not been facing it. That is part of being so busy that you refuse to listen to what you don't want to hear. I responded intuitively. I trusted myself about which markets to focus on to beat my new competitors (my former associates) to the punch. The intuition worked. Things blossomed quickly.

I began to pace myself carefully. I knew that I was in danger of burning out, so I got enthusiastic about looking after me. One of the things that you need to do when things are tight and you are feeling the blues is pamper yourself. So instead of following my urge to beat myself up because of things I felt I hadn't done right, I decided to treat myself right. I frequently filled the bathtub with hot water and took the time to read favorite energy-building books. I went for walks on the beach and through the University of British Columbia's beautiful University Endowment Lands—places that made me feel on top of the world.

I started investing more time in me. I am around a lot of other people who demand my time. They want to take me to lunch and socialize. During this time I did a minimal amount of socializing. Instead, I slipped away to be by myself—in a positive way. I spent time alone and nurtured and developed myself. I built a protection system around myself so I could grow again.

I even went out and bought some angel cards. These are unique little cards with angels on the back of them. You pull one out for the day or for the week, and whatever kind of angel is on the card is the one that's going to be with you. The first one I pulled, for example, was the angel of delight.

unusual support

To use these cards, you think of all the situations ahead of you for the week or the day, and you project that feeling into it—in my case, delight. I tried to get delight into my language. For example, I would begin a speaking engagement by saying "It's a real delight to be here." I'd look at someone who had a really nice outfit on and say, "That's a delightful outfit," or I'd ask people, "Isn't it a delightful day?" All of a sudden there was delight in everything I was doing, and I ran into delightful people everywhere. All this came from a simple little deck of cards called angel cards.

Angel cards may sound a little far out to some of you. Whether or not it is far out doesn't matter; if it works, do it! They helped me change my state of mind. I have given dozens of sets of angel cards to clients all over western Canada. In every case, there is a tray of angel cards in those offices; the staff and customers "lightheartedly" draw an angel for the day.

What was so striking to me about this period of my life was that in time I almost forgot that I had originally felt blue because my close, trustworthy associates left the company and set up in competition. I finally began to realize that there had been problems with these close associates for quite some time and I had refused to look at the situation. It was time for them to go off in their own directions. It provided some fantastic opportunities for me and for some other people involved in my organization who wanted to be there. All of a sudden the original negative influence was a positive.

As a matter of fact, it was the most positive thing that could have happened to me at that time because it forced me to get out in the field and talk to the customers. I once again got in touch with my marketplace and my associates. It forced me to make choices and look beyond my nose. Necessary changes were made with the help of excellent people around me.

The experience also made me ask the all-important question: Do I really want to be in this business, and, if so, what do I want it to be like? I realized that I did want to be here but that over time the actual structure of the company would have to change. My commitment was renewed, and I felt stronger than I had in years. Once again, I was mentally fit and had beaten the blues. I was renewed from the inside out.

Questions to ask yourself:

- Do I dwell on things that hold me back? If so, what are they?
- What can I change in my life to turn these drawbacks into productive assets?
- What are all the things I can be grateful for right now?
- What steps can I take to get both physically and mentally fit?

CHAPTER FOURTEEN

An Inside-Out Summary

The key to a prosperous business in turbulent times—or at any time—is marketing or operating your business from the inside out. Look inside your business. Most people don't recognize the potential power that their businesses already have. You have to know who you are and what you represent before you can market to the outside world.

As we saw in Chapter 9, 68 percent of people don't return to the average place of business because of the attitude of the staff, and 14 percent don't return because of unadjusted complaints. That's 82 percent of business lost because of attitude. The power of any company, any business, any department, any community, and any organization starts with the right attitude. That is why I have focused on getting mentally fit, being enthusiastic, and working from the heart. You can gain 82 percent more business with the right attitude.

Throughout this book I have tried to get you to think like a marketer, a salesperson, and to look for ways to be unique. These things reflect a marketing attitude, and that's what makes people buy from businesses, companies, and individuals. The right attitude is the first and most important power point that you have at your disposal.

The second power point is face-to-face marketing—that is, what happens inside the business (in the store if you are in retail) or outside (when you are making calls, deliveries, or even socializing). The telephone call is part of face-to-face marketing as well. You can advertise all you want, and you can explain who you are and what you do, but when someone actually meets you, the advertising has to match what you are really like. These are the moments of truth.

The third power point is what I call environmental marketing—this is your signage, your point-of-purchase material, your promotional material, your vehicle. It is the design and layout of your business, the displays in your store, and how the business appears.

The fourth power point is extended personal marketing, and this is where direct mail comes in. Direct mail is not categorized with media because it is a little more personal than the media. Direct mail is usually addressed to a specific person, and it's personally signed by the sender. By using direct mail you can extend your personal marketing so that you reach more than one person at the same time in a personal way.

Holding seminars and speaking to groups gives you an opportunity to talk to numerous people at the same time. It is also more personal than a television ad. It is extended personal marketing. Involvement in trade shows and workshops, membership in associations, and devotion of time to the community are also included in the fourth power point of marketing.

The fifth and final power point is media marketing, which includes the use of trade journals, magazines, billboards, brochures, newspapers, television, radio, and other media. The key here is to remember that all these areas of power are important, but the most important part starts on the inside. For example, we have all heard slogans promoting major banks. These slogans say that their mandate is to help small businesses, but often when we get there the bankers are totally unwilling to help. We walk away knowing that those commercials are not true.

If you want your commercials to be really powerful, you've got to make sure that you are marketing from the inside out. Everything from your attitude to your face-to-face marketing to your signage has to match what your media message is saying. Otherwise, you are marketing from the outside in, saying it and not doing it.

Dunsmuir Shell is a good example of marketing from the inside out. If you saw a TV commercial or a newspaper ad that said, "Shell Helps," and you went to the Dunsmuir station, you would truly believe that Shell helps, wouldn't you? Marketing from the inside out does work.

Your real secret weapon, however, in marketing and operating your business is not usually your media, community work, physical factors, or even your sales skills. It is the attitude of you and your people. The right attitude doesn't cost a penny, it's something that other companies can't track or copy, and it will propel your business to new heights, especially in turbulent times. During such unstable times you must always stay focused. You may not have the money to spend on the media, but you can pool your resources and get out and build the company from the inside out.

All of the ideas in this book can be placed within the Marketing From The Inside Out Model (see Figure 14.1). I've been speaking on this model since Neil Godin and I came up with a similar concept ten years ago. Business can be profitable and fun if you stick to the basics of inside-out marketing.

Bill Gibson's Marketing From The Inside Out Model

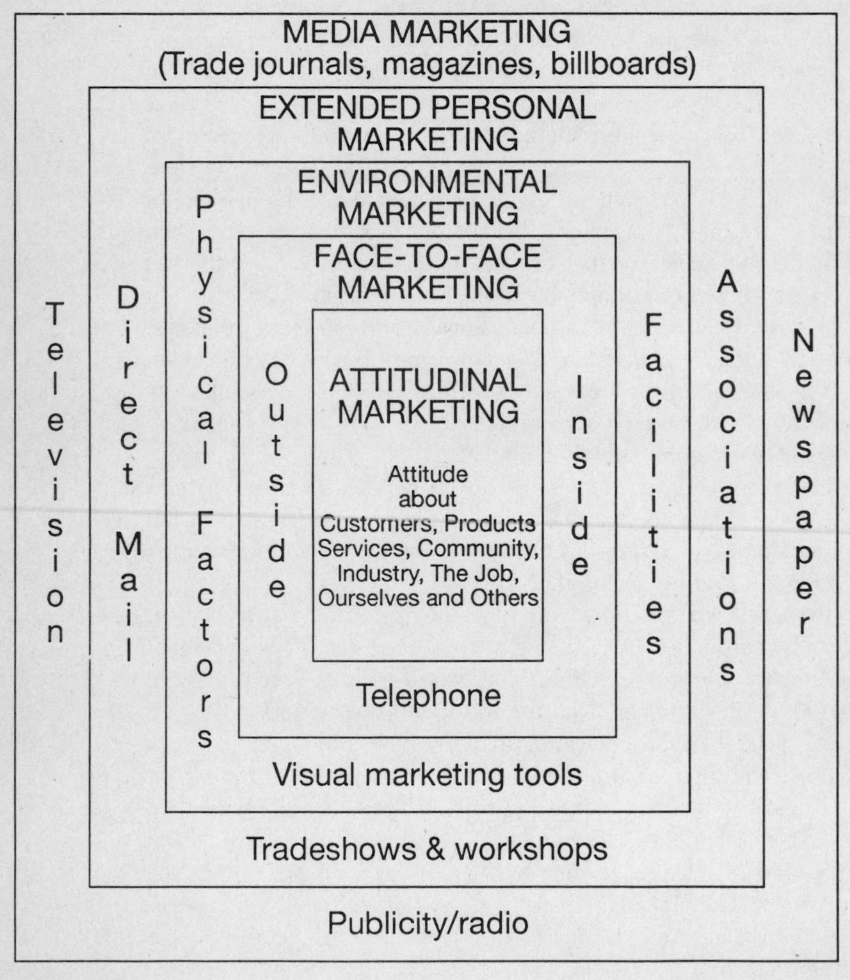

Figure 14.1

Read this daily and *do* it:

- If not now, when?
- If not me, who?
- If not this way, what way?

And remember, boldness produces miracles.

About the Author

Bill Gibson has spoken to over 700,000 people throughout North America. He is an entrepreneur, a marketing person, an author, and the founder of the Newport Business Owner Development programs. With over 6,000 business owners graduating from his ten-month owner training programs, Bill has become one of North America's leading specialists in both small and large business training.

His eighteen years of practical experience as a business owner and the "real life" stories from his clients gives him a never-ending supply of usable ideas and methods to succeed in business. He is down-to-earth, entertaining, and results-oriented.

Bill is the President and CEO of The Bill Gibson Group Inc. and Newport Marketing & Communications Inc. of Vancouver, British Columbia, and was born and raised in a small Nova Scotia community on the East Coast of Canada. He now resides in beautiful British Columbia with his wife Beverley and two sons, Ryan and Shane.

His clients include such companies as AT&T, Jim Pattison Group, GTE, Mobil Chemical Canada, Commonwealth Holiday Inns, National Association of Insurance Women, Canadian National Institute for the Blind, Chamber of Commerce Executives of Canada, Credit Union Executive Society, Great American Insurance Co., California Blue Shield, The CHUM Group, Canada Employment and Immigration, and a host of others.

FREE OFFER – Audio Tape of Bill Gibson Live

To receive a free copy of this audio tape please complete the following Reader Comment Form and mail or fax to:

Bill Gibson
c/o Newport Marketing & Communications Inc.
Suite 750 - 1155 W. Pender Street, Vancouver, B.C., CANADA V6E 2P4
Vancouver Area: (604) 684-1211, Toll Free: 1-800-663-0336 (USA & Canada)
Fax: (604) 684-1209

Name:____________________ Date:__________

Company Name:____________________

Company address:____________________

City:__________ State/Province:__________ Postal Code__________

Telephone:__________ Fax:__________ Size of Company (# of employees) ☐ Under 15 ☐ 16-50 ☐ 51-100 ☐ 101-500 ☐ 501+

Your Position:____________________

Male ☐ Female ☐ Age: Under 18 ☐ 18-29 ☐ 30-39 ☐ 40-49 ☐ 50-59 ☐ 60+ ☐

How would you rate the basic content ☐ Excellent ☐ Good ☐ Fair ☐ Poor

How would you rate Bill's writing style ☐ Excellent ☐ Good ☐ Fair ☐ Poor

Please express your overall feeling about the Boost Your Business in Any Economy Book:

____

____

____

Please indicate the topics you'd like to see Bill Gibson expand upon in other books.

- ☐ Commando thinking
- ☐ Sales excellence
- ☐ Customer service
- ☐ Hiring & keeping good people
- ☐ Effective advertising
- ☐ Balancing business & personal life
- ☐ Mentally fit
- ☐ Problem solving
- ☐ Finding business opportunities
- ☐ Marketing from the inside-out
- ☐ Financially fit
- ☐ Non-traditional planning
- ☐ Other ____________________

Please contact me re:

- ☐ Bill Gibson speaking for an association I am a member of
- ☐ Bill Gibson training or speaking within our company
- ☐ Information about Bill Gibson's video based training material
- ☐ Information about other audio tapes and books
- ☐ Employee and entrepreneurial assessment tools

Please sign your name if you permit Bill to use your comments in his promotional materials.

____

Thank you for taking the time to help us with our research.
1 tape per person, please.

INDEX

A

Advertising strategies, 14–18, 99–115
Advo, 37
Air Canada, 90
American Express, 37, 104, 108
Analyzing business problems, 45–50
AT&T, 44
Axciom, 36–37

B

Batting, Rick, 129
B.C. Tel, 70
Beveridge, Ron, 65
Bidewell, Ron, 93
Brainstorming, 23–25
Brick, The, 16–17, 20–21
Bridgeport Carpets, 92–93, 104

C

Canador College, 59
Capitalizing on a problem, 1
Cauvier, Dennis, 161
Century 21 Canada, 49
CFAX Radio, 129
CFDR Radio, 69
Charlottetown Hotel, 92
Chase Manhattan Bank, 37
CHNS Radio, 69
Chrysler Corporation, 7
CHUM Group of Companies, 69
Citerilla, Joseph, 55
Citicorp, 37
CJCH Radio, 54, 69
CJCH Television, 103
Clearbrook Photographic, 63
Commando thinking, 51–59
Confederation College, 59
Cooper, Mel, 129
Customer relations, 14–16, 25–26, 55–57, 77–81, 87–98
Cutty Sark, 115
Cycles, economic, 2–12

D

Davidson, Betty, 71
Davidson, Bob, 71–72, 161
Decision making, 123–25
Despy Manufacturing, 123
Digger's Roadhouse, 23
Doule, Randy, 103
Drew, Dick, 144
Dunsmuir, Bob, 79–85, 92, 132, 134
Dunsmuir Shell, 77–85, 92, 165

E

Economic cycles, 2–12
Employee relations, 23–25, 80–86, 125–29
Esso Home Comfort, 104
Express Services, 119

F

Financial management, 128–43
  banker relationships, 128–32
  budgeting, 132–34

Financial management *(continued)*
collecting money, 138–42
dealing with debt, 142
saving money, 135–38
Fisher Nuts, 115
Forty Winks Waterbeds, 13–20, 28, 55, 62, 100, 102, 105
Fraser Valley College, 59
Fulfillment Corp. of America, 37
Funk, Bob, 119

G

General Motors, 44
Gibson, Beverley, 30, 74, 78, 87, 118, 144–45, 147, 150, 160–61
Gibson, Robyn, 116
Gibson, Ryan, 144–45, 147, 150
Gibson, Shane, 8–9, 60–61, 116, 144–45, 147, 150
Gibson-Shaw, Rick, 39, 66, 161
Glynmill Inn, 89–90, 92
Godin, Neil, 2–3, 70, 89, 93, 165
Grey, Peter, 161
Gunn, Barry, 23
Gwynne-Timothy, John, 103

H

Harris Electric, 25
Herzberg Theory of Management, 80–83
Hillside Antiques, 118
HMV Canada, 5–6
Holly Tree Place, 63
Hudson, John, 136
Humphrey, George, 6
Husky Oil, 120

I

IBM, 27, 40, 44
Inside-out marketing, 164–67
Ioannou, Greg, 26

J

Jordan, Herb, 69

K

Kelly's Stereo Mart, 103
Kilby, Norm, 137
Kotow, Joe, 96–97
Krotz, Vicki, 19–22, 27, 94
Kubas, Len, 6

L

Langdon, Chuck, 54
Lawrie, Marilyn, 137
Lazer Data Graphics, 136
Lean and keen management, 116–27
Lee, Greg, 103
Leonard, Stu, 25
Lucky Dollar stores, 51–53

M

MacLeod, George, 69
Maloney, Steve, 161
Maloney, Tim, 161
Management Recruiters International, 41
Marketing strategies, 19–21, 99–115
inside-out, 164–67
McKay, Joe, 1–2

McNeil, Ken, 87–88
Meeting Planners International, 64
Mental fitness, 144–63
  anxiety reduction, 145, 149–57
  dealing with creditors, 158–59
  problem solving, 157–58
  thinking positively, 159–62
  time management, 145–48
Merry, Chelsea, 145
Merry, Gordon, 145
Merry, Kiersten, 145
Merry, Lil, 145
Midas Mufflers, 48–49
Morgan, Charles, Jr., 36–37
Mount Saint Helens, 11

N

Nelson Building Supplies, 120
Nelson Homes, 120
Nelson, Irv, 117–18, 135
Newport Marketing and
    Communications, Inc., 45–47,
    49, 57, 59, 64, 72, 74, 87
New Tread Tires, 113
Nightingale, Earl, 149

P

Pals, Mike, 161
Penn Central Railroad, 7
Port Alberni, B.C., 2–3

R

Reger, Jim, 30
Reid, Sharon, 145
Research, market, 23–25,
    106–7
Robbins, Anthony, 158
Royal Bank of Canada, 28, 108
Royal Canadian Mounted Police, 28
Royal Ford, 97
Rusnell, Dale, 39

S

Sam the Record Man, 5
Scarboro Fair Fashions, 19–21, 28,
    94
Selling techniques, 39, 60–76
  business cards, use of, 62–63
  closing sales, 73–74
  generating leads, 63–64, 69
  networking, 68
  obtaining referrals, 64–66
  qualifying buyers, 72–73
  telephone strategies, 66–68
Shell Canada, 83, 92
Sherman, Gordon, 48–49
Sherry's Sweet Shop, 23
Simpson, Andrew, 63
Small, Brian, 64
Snapshot, Thirty-Minute, 45–50
Sports on Broadway, 115
Stages of business growth, 30–44
  existence, 31–33, 38–40, 42
  resource maturity, 31, 38, 40–41,
    44
  Success D, 31, 33–35, 40–43
  Success G, 31, 33–35, 40–43, 46
  survival, 31, 33, 39–40, 42–44
  takeoff, 30–31, 35–41, 43–44,
    46
Stallone, Salvatore, 18
Stallone, Sylvester, 18
Stephens, Inc., 36–37
Stoller, Bill, 119
Straker, Corrine, 13, 16, 20, 55, 136
Straker, Terry, 13–22, 55, 62, 102, 105,
    136, 161
Straker, Zack, 17

T

Texaco, 85
Thomas, Peter, 49, 125
Toronto-Dominion Bank, 129
Tourism Newfoundland, 90
Triple-A Employment, 97

V

Vance, Michael, 94

W

Webb, Dennis, 18, 20
Wightman, Reg, 62
Wood Motors Ford, 103
Woolco, 82